re:F🗘RM

Patrick A. Hegarty

HEGARTY.COM.AU

AUSTRALIA

CONTENTS

Introduction

FOR OVER A DECADE I focused on unlocking the spiritual health and vibrancy of believers, and identifying the reasons why they might get stuck.

There remains so much at stake in this regard.

The world has never ceased yearning for the demonstrable truth about eternity. They are looking for answers, and for people who demonstrate what they claim.

Christians hold those answers.

Yet, if we are as locked down in our dysfunction, brokenness, addictions and idolatry as the world is, then we have no moral authority. Even worse, we lack the power that is so clearly demonstrated and accepted as normal in the New Testament.

The most significant difference in the potential of a Christian versus a non-believer is the presence of God's Spirit within us.

And yet very few know how to partner with Him in a way that overcomes sin and gives a grand vision for life.

This material gives to you some proven keys in how to do that.

Having taken thousands of people through these principles, and seen the vast majority of those lives transformed significantly, I have no doubt that anyone can change with God's help.

His offer is Shalom – peace. Peace within your soul despite the circumstance. Peace with God, peace with yourself, peace with others and peace with your world.

His offer is also power – power to be healed, and to go and heal the world.

Is that your story yet? It can be.

God is determined to re:FORM you.

He does it through inviting you into deeper union with Him. And as you contemplate His glory, you are changed to reflect that, going from glory to ever-increasing glory.

Over the next six weeks, God will lead you deeper into an experience of repentance and belief. Enjoy that journey, and determine to come through the other side free of those things which bind you.

Patrick Hegarty

Using this material

MEET TOGETHER WEEKLY

This material is designed to be done with others. There are six readings per week, followed by a group session. Group sessions are great settings to share and process your responses to daily content.

DIGEST THE CONTENT DAILY

Read a single chapter per day, and invest time thinking about your response. Read the scripture verses mentioned at the beginning of each chapter, before working through each day's content.

ATTEND A SPIRITUAL RETREAT

Completion of chapter 2.6 (ending week 2) is an effective moment to run a spiritual retreat. There participants can pause to receive ministry, and process deeply the concepts before contemplating change. Resources for hosting a spiritual retreat are available at www.hegarty.com.au.

Group Session 1

INTRODUCTIONS

Spend some time going around the group, hearing the names, family details and life context of each participant.

Q. What would you like to get from this course?

_____

_____

ABOUT re:FORM

Read together:

Welcome to re:FORM. This material is all about equipping you to become what the apostle Paul called the spiritual person (1 Corinthians 3:1; Greek: *pneumatikos*).

The great majority of Christians believe they are spiritually mature but, in reality, experience little of the empowering presence of God in their daily lives. We don't become mature simply by doing the Christian life for years, or by behaving like a nice person.

Being a spiritual person is about living with the power of God working through us, activated in an intimate and dynamic relationship with our God. 1 Corinthians 4:20 confirms that the *"kingdom of God is not a matter of talk, but of power"*.

Becoming spiritual seldom happens by accident. To grow, we need to engage with God through a deliberate rhythm of grace called "Repentance and Belief". This material will equip you to do just that. You will be able to identify an area of your life where you need the Spirit's help to overcome, and to work through the process to being spirit-empowered.

How to go through material:

There are six daily readings per week to process and respond to. Do one per day only as you will need to meditate on and process the concepts slowly. Fill in the *Your response* section slowly, reflectively and honestly, or you won't receive the full benefit of the process.

In your group meetings your facilitator will help you process and apply the week's concepts.

GROUP AGREEMENT

For your group to be safe and effective, you will need to agree on how you will interact and honour each other. Talk through together which boundaries you may want to have in place for the duration of the course. Below are some suggestions and you can add your own.

GROUP ATTENDANCE

We will honour each other by being on time and regularly attending meetings.

SAFE ENVIRONMENT

We will create a place where each person is protected and loved, free to share without judgment or unsolicited advice.

RESPECT DIFFERENCES

We will be gentle and gracious to those with different spiritual maturity, opinions and temperaments.

CONFIDENTIALITY

What is said in the group stays in the group.

FAITHFULNESS

We will diligently engage with the material, processing our responses honestly.

OTHER POINTS OF IMPORTANCE

_____

_____

_____

_____

_____

_____

_____

YOUR SPIRITUAL JOURNEY SO FAR

Q: Can you describe what it is like for you to be empowered by God's Spirit in some area of your life?

_____

_____

Q. What is an area where you have seen the most obvious change in your life since you met Christ?

_____

_____

_____

Q. What factors contributed to that transformation?

_____

_____

_____

Q. If you could identify a few key things that have incited you to grow spiritually, what would they be?

_____

_____

_____

Q. Might there have been a better or more effective way to grow in that area?

_____

_____

PRAY FOR EACH OTHER

Take some time discussing the prayer needs of each person in the group and how best you will support them this week.

_____

_____

_____

_____

_____

_____

_____

_____

_____

_____

_____

_____

_____

_____

_____

_____

_____

_____

Finish the meeting by having the group all stand in a circle. Then take turns having the others lay hands on them, praying that God would answer their prayers and hopes.

Come to life

READ FIRST: GENESIS 1:1–2:7

You are not an accident. You have been designed ... created to live.

The detail of who you are has been in the mind of God since before time. From His heart of unlimited love, He called you into being for this very moment, to take your place in His story. Your story is part of His story.

His is an endless mosaic of all the colours of His love. He created all things, with intricate order and unbreakable laws. Yet He wove within that the potential for the imperfect to somehow co-exist with the perfect. Even our failure provides an opportunity for His redemption to reveal more of His love.

You were designed to be with Him. The very fabric of your being is meant to be woven together with the presence of God. Jesus said it like this, *"Father, just as you are in me and I am in you. May they also be in us ..."*[1]

You are never alone – never lost – never abandoned.

The creation story in Genesis 2:7 tells us why.

> *"Then the LORD God formed a man from the dust of the ground and breathed into his nostrils the breath of life, and the man became a living being."*

Dust and breath. We are made of both elements.

The dust is the stuff of this earth. We are physical beings, limited in resources and confined to time and space.

And yet we have breath – God's eternal breath. *Pneuma*[2].

Humans did not live until the breath of life was given to them. We are in that respect uniquely made for eternity. The dust is nothing without the breath, and we are nothing without God's powerful presence bringing and sustaining life every moment.

Sometimes we are aware of it. We recognise that His powerful hand sustains us and gives us what we need. But too often we act like we are alone. We reason from our own logic, work from our own resource, strive to be someone who makes things happen.

This is what the bible calls being worldly. It is the logic of spiritual babies, the Apostle Paul says. In 1 Corinthians 3:1 he says to a group of obviously saved people that *"I could not address you as people who live by the Spirit but as people who are still worldly – mere infants in Christ"*.

Paul never did hold back from telling it how it is. He knew that anything less than life by the Spirit was a rejection of what the cross had made possible – a life here and now with the breath of God in our lungs.

The interesting thing is that these believers thought they were doing pretty well to this point. They believed in Christ, got baptised, came together for church meetings – many of the things we would say proved they were dwelling with Christ.

They were doing the stuff, but they weren't being the stuff. They were not living from the Spirit of God.

When Jesus rose from the dead, the first thing He did was find the disciples and release this ability to breathe again. In John 20:22 He entered the room and breathed on them saying, *"Receive the sacred breath"*, referring to the Holy Spirit.

Jesus had earlier said, *"I have come that you may have life, and have it to the full"*[3].

This full life is only found in being dust and breath. To live from dust is a half-life – it's doing it in your own strength, trying to be good enough on your own, doing it the world's way. Doing it as if Jesus never went to the cross.

Dwell on that for a moment.

The single biggest difference between those who had faith in God's redemption before the cross and those with faith after the cross is the presence of God's indwelling Spirit.

We have within us that which all those believers would have longed for – God with us, Emmanuel. We have permission to live as both dust and breath. We can commune with God, breathe in His grace, and find peace and victory regardless of the circumstance.

But so often we don't, do we?

We nod our head at the idea of empowerment but the practice can seem far off.

Christian men find themselves seemingly unable to break the addictive grip of pornography in the same proportion as those who do not know Christ. Their shame weighs heavily, their defeat seems inevitable, and their hopelessness becomes profound.

Christian women, too, bear relentless pain. So many have their sense of acceptance fueled in a shallow way by the approving glances of others. Enormous amounts of time, money and energy will be spent to compete for approval and aim for perfection. They size each other up – judging, comparing, feeling good or bad about themselves.

These are examples of worldly thinking and worldly fruit. It is the life of dust in the absence of breath.

Your ability to breathe in Christ is determined by how clogged your spiritual lungs are by the world's lies and brokenness. This course is all about helping you breathe. It is about showing you how to clear your lungs and come to life, perhaps for the first time.

This is a key moment in the spiritual maturity of every believer, one we must all traverse. And one that we all revisit continually.

When we place our faith in Christ, we receive His Spirit within – we are born again[4]. But we must learn how to engage with Him, to partner with Him, and to rely on Him for the grace we need.

This is the journey from being worldly to becoming spiritual – the *pneumatikos*. You don't do it by trying harder or doing better. That has never worked – it didn't work before Christ and it doesn't work now. Christ didn't die so you could work harder; He died so that you would have redemptive access to Him through the Spirit.

He died so that you would live. He died so you could finally breathe again. So begin now by breathing Him in and receiving His life. By faith we have everything we need in Christ.

PRAYER

Lord, I invite and breathe in the fullness of your presence with me now. Without your Spirit I am but dust.

Help me today to be mindful of your presence and ever-hungry for more of your power in my life. I believe your promise of an abundant life. Lead me in to more of that today.

Amen.

REFERENCES

1. John 17:21
2. *Pneuma* – Greek for breath, or spirit. In the New Testament this word is used to describe the Spirit of God.
3. John 10:10
4. 2 Corinthians 1:22

YOUR RESPONSE

What is your response to this offer of life? Is this what you want? Do you yearn for relief from the agendas of this world and the need to do well or look good? Spend a few minutes writing down your response and desire for God at the beginning of this course. At the end, things may well look very different for you.

_____

_____

_____

_____

_____

_____

_____

_____

_____

_____

_____

_____

_____

1.2

Called

Abram had followed God for years ... 24 long years.

Back then Abram had been given a promise from God – a picture of how things would turn out. A calling.

He had been promised that a nation would come from him, a huge family that would go on to bless the world. Abram believed that promise and had lived all this time in waiting. But after 24 years all he had to show was his own failed attempts at bringing about God's will.

He had been promised a son, but no son had come. His wife was barren and so eventually Abram had tried to do it his own way. He had slept with his maidservant and she gave birth to a boy, Ishmael. But God's call had to be done God's way, through Abram's wife Sarai.

And so Abram continued to wait. And while he waited Abram got on with life. He made a living, loved his wife, built his herds and made a name for himself. But something had happened in those 24 years that Abram hadn't noticed.

He had *become* God's calling.

Calling was not what he was to do. Nor would his calling be fulfilled merely by building a family. Abram was looking to what happened on the outside and had missed what had happened on the inside. But it was the inside that God was interested in. Abram himself was to become the calling.

After 24 years God again came to Abram and said, *"No longer will you be called Abram; your name will be Abraham, for I have made you a father of many nations"*. (Genesis 17:5)

Did you get that? God said, *"I **have** made you"*.

He didn't say, *"Now you can go and **do** my calling"*. He was saying that Abram had become the calling, and that calling was to be a father of many nations. That was who Abram had become on the inside, so now the outside would naturally follow suit.

Back then your name represented who you were – your character and destiny. God had morphed a man's apparent destiny from being the father of a household (Abram) to being a father of nations (Abraham). And God had done that subversively over those years.

In Isaiah 43:1, God echoes this form of calling saying, *"Do not fear, for I have redeemed you, I have called you by name"*.

His destiny for your life is brought about by Him morphing your character. Your inner world holds the secrets to who you are and what you will ultimately become.

By dealing with your inner world, God brings about His plans for you. And your outer world will always ultimately reflect the state of your inner world. Only once he had become the father of nations did Abraham eventually give birth to his son Isaac.

The world may define you by your appearance or performance, but not God. He doesn't have a mind for all that. He is going for your heart because your heart belongs to Him.

Everything that is external and temporal will fade away, but not your heart. And God is only concerned with what is eternal.

"And now these three remain: faith, hope and love"[1]. Those three things remain forever, and so God is relentlessly at work in you, digging deep so you can find your faith, hope and love in Him.

We want our needs answered *by* Him. But He first wants our needs to be met *in* Him.

We think spiritual maturity is living *for* God. He sees maturity in those who live *from* God.

This is the *pneumatikos* – the one who lives as dust and breath. Paul unveiled this glorious mystery when he declared the simple dynamic as *"Christ in you, the hope of glory"*[2].

The spiritual person that Paul describes, the *pneumatikos*, is one who knows how to partner fully with God. To do this, you need to know what your part to play is, and what is God's.

Some come at it assuming we have no role to play at all. They say that we are wretched, worthless and sinners to the core ... that there is nothing we can do that is of any value, it is all up to God. And they can point you to verses to that end. But let me save you the trouble of looking them up, just go straight to Romans 7:24 which says, *"What a wretched man I am!"*

In fact, the whole of Romans 7 is a litany of catchphrases and defeatist statements that mourn the reality that *"what I want to do I do not do, but what I hate I do!"*

The reality is, however, that the author, Paul, is writing in the past tense. He is saying that, as one who strived to follow the law, it was impossible for him. But then in Romans 8 he celebrates the fact that with Christ in his life he is free from the law and can now fully live in Christ. The point is, he is no better than he was before but now he has Christ and can live!

When we have a low value of humanity – one which is well below the value that God sets on us – we tend to deny all of who we are in a form of defacing humility. We say, *"I must decrease so that He may increase"*[3]. Again, this is a misquotation of John the Baptist who was saying that it was time for his light to dim so that the ministry of Jesus could get more recognition.

Let's be real clear about this – God doesn't want less of you; He wants all of you!

He made you, He designed you, He loves you ... completely, and as you are! The Psalms say that you are *"fearfully and wonderfully made"*[4].Most of us have never seen the fullness of who God has made us to be because we are either too busy trying to be who the world wants us to be, or we are trying to put ourselves "to death" in some form of fake spiritual discipline.

But God doesn't want you dead, He wants you fully alive! That's why Jesus said, *"I have come that you may have life, and life to the full"*[5].

What needs to be put aside is your old carnal nature, that part of you that brings death and unhealthy brokenness.

When God calls you by name, He is calling out the gold He sees in you – the gold He Himself has placed in you. He knows that if your old nature is swept away, and the nature He created to be in union with Him comes to life, then you will fully live as you should.

If you try telling Him how wretched you are, you will find God doesn't engage in that conversation. He doesn't agree with you!

He is dealing with you in accordance with who He believes you will become. And so God relentlessly deals with us from this perspective. He is very patient and He will not short-cut the plan He has for your life.

I wonder what He is dealing with in you? I wonder what is getting in the way of His best for you. Best to let Him deal with it, because He will not be changing His mind on who He believes you should be.

PRAYER

Today Lord I choose to believe that you are not finished with me. You have plans for good, fruit to bear, dreams to give and see fulfilled.

I leave behind the mistakes of the past, as you have. I look instead to the hope I have in Christ, a hope based in what you give me.

Begin to show me what is in the way of that promised life and lead me in the way everlasting.

Amen

REFERENCES

1. 1 Corinthians 13:13
2. Colossians 1:27
3. John 3:30
4. Psalm 139:14
5. John 10:10

YOUR RESPONSE

What has God been dealing with in your life? Does any area continually come up as a problem? If you had to guess, what do you think you need to put to death so you can fully live?

_____

_____

_____

_____

_____

_____

_____

_____

_____

_____

_____

_____

_____

_____

_____

_____

_____

_____

_____

_____

_____

_____

_____

_____

_____

_____

_____

_____

_____

_____

_____

_____

_____

1.3

What owns you?

READ FIRST: ROMANS 6

Have you ever indulged in a moment where you looked at your life from an outside perspective?

By that I mean that you pause to consider where you have come from; where you are heading; and, if you dare to ask it, why you are heading that way at all.

You may ask, How did it all come to this? What drove me to choose this path? Why do I keep making the same mistakes with people and life choice? Why am I so driven to achieve, and why do I judge so harshly those who are weaker than I am?

We may go months, maybe years, without asking these sorts of questions at any depth. And so, many times a day we may be asked, "How are you?" and we answer, "Fine thanks, and you?"

On a surface level we are probably being honest. Most days we are doing well enough. We have our routine, our circles of friends, our ways of engaging with life. "It's not perfect", we think, "but it's fine".

Is it really fine? By what standard are we measuring "fine"? Usually it is in comparison with everyone else – our friends, peers and cultural standards. We may even compare with other nations poorer than ours and be thankful that our life is so much easier than theirs.

The scriptures, however, draw from a different measurement.

1 Peter 2:9 says that *"You are a chosen people, a royal priesthood, a holy nation, God's special possession"*. You are from God's nation, His people. You are royalty in the most profound and eternal sense. Like it or not, you are not like other people.

You are chosen. You have been specifically called. You have been singled out for a valuable purpose. That means our comparative view on how we are doing is not valid. Only God's view is valid. And His calling on you means you are being ever-developed into someone more glorious.

To make you into the person God has in mind, He will relentlessly seek to weed out those elements of your life that don't reflect that design. They are the "old you", the elements that came from wrong choices, a wounded heart, or the damage inflicted from our less-than-perfect beginnings.

They are the things that hold you back – and they might also be the things that drive you forward, sometimes in directions that bring you harm.

In that sense, we could call them slave drivers. Their presence in our life controls our actions – often unconsciously. Slave drivers are relentless and cruel. They don't protect us or seek our good, they simply control us.

Some slave drivers may appear by worldly standards to be our friends. A drive to achieve can result in great wealth. The drive to control may result in people doing what we want. The rewards are always fleeting, however, and often result from the pain or devaluing of others. These are not the rewards or values that interest God.

Most of our slave drivers come in the form of an inner, hidden and nameless pain. And pain always seeks pleasure. So we act out in a way that may ultimately do us harm, yet offer momentary relief. We may push away those who get too close. We might develop addictions to things like drugs, pornography, food, even shopping – desperate to have just a moment of pleasure rather than residual turmoil. Our drivers compel us to avoid our fears, cloak our wounds, cover our imperfection and avoid dealing with lifelong dysfunction.

This then becomes our idea of "fine".

But it isn't fine, is it?

Paul talked about us serving our old nature in Romans 6:16 saying, *"Don't you know that when you offer yourselves to someone as obedient slaves, you are slaves of the one you obey"*.

One thing is certain – you are not called or obliged to be a slave of sin. Paul goes on to say in Romans 8 that *"we have an obligation ... but it is not to the flesh, to live according to it ... The Spirit you received does not make you slaves, so that you live in fear again; rather, the Spirit you received brought about your adoption to sonship"*.

In practice, however, many good Christian people do in fact feel like slaves, unable to control the darker areas of their life. And so these areas remain hidden from view in the hope that they won't be found out, won't need to be dealt with, and won't bring shame upon us.

Sadly, however, what you cannot talk about will inevitably own you. That which remains hidden becomes a slave driver. But Jesus died so that you would be free – totally free.

Our slave drivers are the deep-rooted issues that prevent us fulfilling our calling in Christ. They are the parts of our old nature that clog our spiritual lungs and restrict us breathing in the fullness of Christ.

Any thorough discussion about living under the full influence of God's Spirit will include the topic of dealing with our old nature. Sadly, though, we too often restrict this conversation to telling people to just stop sinning. We implore them that God is good, they are bad, and that they need to try much harder.

This just doesn't work. It didn't work in the Old Testament and it sure doesn't work in the New Testament either. Sin is usually the result of something deeper. Sin can be likened to bad fruit; if it is cut off it will always return unless the underlying issue is resolved. When you see the fruit, always look for the root. Once we deal with the roots of sin in our life, the fruit is so much easier to eradicate.

Much of this course is written to restore and build hope for God's people. Hopelessness comes when we feel powerless to overcome, or lose a sense of divine purpose. Our fears, shame and brokenness destroy hope for a better day.

You are about to be equipped in how to break through. The tools you learn in this course can be used for your whole life and will serve you well in overcoming all sorts of dysfunction and pain.

But first, we must shine a light on that pain. We will expose gently what is hidden so that you lose your slave drivers. We will expose some of the lies you have believed so that, as Jesus promised, *"the truth will set you free"*.

PRAYER

Lord, I recognise that there are some areas of my life where you are not in control. I no longer want to behave like a slave, driven by anything other than your grace.

Please show me the thing you are giving me grace and opportunity to deal with in this season.

Amen.

REFERENCES

1. John 8:32

YOUR RESPONSE

1. Read Exodus 3:7–8

2. God hears the cry of those who are controlled by negative influences, and wants to bring freedom.

3. Go to **Appendix 1 – Spiritual Health Assessment**. Fill in the survey slowly and honestly, looking to identify some of the common areas (or slave drivers) in which many past participants of this material have found significant transformation.

4. Then reflect here on the following:

What is the most consistent issue that you battle with in life, that you know is holding you back or limiting your spiritual growth?

_____

_____

_____

_____

Is there a particular fear, addiction, relational dysfunction, shame or other consistent issue that you struggle to control?

_____

_____

_____

_____

What is it that you consistently do that you know is not God's plan for you?

_____

_____

_____

_____

1.4

Afraid and alone

READ FIRST: GENESIS 3

The man was completely disorientated and uncomfortable – feelings he had never known in his life before this moment.

He had never experienced anything but completeness, had never felt this awkward sense of inadequacy and fear. He felt alone for the first time, like something or someone had been ripped from his life, leaving a gaping chasm in his thoughts, emotions and plans.

He was Adam, the first human being. He had been created from dust and breath – formed from the substance of temporal earth, but empowered and sustained from the eternal God. But that had just been changed forever.

He had that day chosen independence, determined to judge for himself what was right and wrong. In that single act, Adam had divorced himself from God, tearing violently apart a union of spirit that had been woven into the deepest fabric of his life.

As he locked eyes with his wife Eve, they must have seen the mutual horror that now pervaded their souls. They were together and yet deeply alone – isolated from their common life source, the Lord God who had both created and loved them.

The vacuum they discovered in their inner worlds still exists by default in every single human being who has been born since that moment. It is the greatest tragedy in the cosmos – the fall of humankind, as described in Genesis 3.

We all share their deficit and pain but, since it is all we have known, it feels a lot more normal than it did to Adam and Eve. We have had thousands of years of practice at filling that void. We have replaced God with idols – slave drivers that control us in the place of a loving God who invites us to life. We claim to be free, but unredeemed humanity is in reality captive to the inner emptiness they long to fill.

An idol is really anything that you defer to or consult rather than God.

They determine our choices and therefore are as powerful as our slave drivers. Materialism, for example, is an idol. We know we only need so many possessions to live safely and well, and yet we constantly spend our money on that which simply adds more. And even when we inevitably become aware of the needs of the poor, and our capacity to give, we look first to our idol. It tells us that if we give that money we won't be able to have that other thing – the thing we "need".

Idols take all sorts of shapes. Adam and Eve found theirs almost immediately – we might call it *approval*. They would bow to that idol, as multitudes do today, for the rest of their lives.

Adam and Eve's first reaction was to seek approval, to compensate for their new-found insecurity. Approval had previously come from God; now they looked for it from each other and themselves.

"The eyes of both of them were opened, and they realised they were naked; so they sewed fig leaves together and made coverings for themselves". Genesis 3:7

How different was this from the scene before this in Genesis 2:25, *"Adam and Eve were both naked and were not ashamed"*.

They were no less beautiful than they were a few minutes before, but now they had assumed the role of judge, and in assessing themselves by their own standard they got it hugely wrong. They believed a lie about themselves and deferred immediately to their new self-sourced replacement for God. They covered their nakedness to hide from each other, then, just as foolishly, found cover from which to hide from God.

Our coverings don't change anything, they just attempt to hide things and thus avoid shame. It's strange that when we sense an internal vacuum we look for external solutions. But a vacuum needs to be filled. You were designed to be filled with the Presence of God, bringing a union that provides security, acceptance, identity, courage and purpose. Nothing else can sufficiently meet those needs.

Idols are the tangible representation of our slave drivers. Adam and Eve's idol of approval was the outworking of deeper slave drivers like shame, fear and inadequacy.

If only these idols would just stay on the shelf inanimately! But in our unredeemed state they are constantly with us, promising to fill the void left by God's presence and grace. They all come from one over-arching condition, one we could call an *orphaned spirit*.

An orphan is one who is abandoned and alone, and orphaned is the way Adam and Eve felt when God's presence left them. They were no longer "dust and breath"; now they were just dust. This dry and defenceless state relentlessly looks for filling and fulfilment in the absence of God. Sadly, many find just enough of that temporary fulfilment to numb themselves to the availability of God Himself.

Just as we chose to be alone, so we can choose to be complete again. Jesus' death on the cross paid the price we could never pay for our sin. That death made union with God possible again to all who would seek it; all the hindrances were removed and the veil of separation made redundant.

Jesus said, *"I will not leave you as orphans, but I will come to you"* (John 14:18). He was referring to the presence of God in the form of His Spirit dwelling within you. You are no longer merely dust. You are dust and breath! All your needs can validly and tangibly be found again through your union with God.

This union – this intimacy – is available to you, and yet it is not automatic.

Too few Christians understand this. They live as largely atheistic believers, a paradox where we believe in God without relying on Him for the power we need. We claim to be alive in Christ because we believe in and follow Him, and yet we still defer to idols such as fear and shame in the same way that unbelievers do.

Paul describes it this way in 1 Corinthians 3:1, *"I could not address you as people who live by the Spirit but as people who are still worldly – mere infants in Christ"*.

To be spiritual is to be driven by the Spirit of God. We are not who God is determined we become until we are driven by the power of our relationship with Him. We grow more spiritual by putting to death the old nature, idol by dol.

This material will help you identify your idols, both hidden and obvious. It is time for you to come to life. Invite God to help you on that journey, shining a light on every dark place. You have nothing to lose and everything to gain.

PRAYER

Lord, I thank you that I am never an orphan. You are always with me and I am never alone. Your help is always there and your love always gives me what I need.

I admit that sometimes I still feel alone and afraid, but help me to see and believe the truth of your closeness and affection for me. I choose to believe what you have said and done for me.

Amen

YOUR RESPONSE

Look over leaf at the list of common modern-day idols and mark those that you either:

- consider when making decisions
- use to feel significant
- get more passionate or excited about than God
- use as source of security
- look to in determining your future direction.

OUR 21ST CENTURY IDOLS

Mark those that are present in your life:

Sport	☐	Body image	☐
Fashion	☐	Appearance	☐
Success	☐	Materialism	☐
Power	☐	Approval	☐
Control	☐	Independence	☐
Significance	☐	Individualism	☐
Comfort	☐	Money	☐
Entitlement	☐	Recognition	☐

Have another idol in your life? List it here.

_____

_____

_____

_____

_____

_____

For more in-depth and comprehensive background on idols in our culture, refer to the material by Timothy Keller. In particular:

Keller, T. 2010, *The Gospel in Life: Grace Changes Everything*, Zondervan.

Keller, T. 2011, *Counterfeit Gods*, Penguin Putnam Inc.

1.5

Corrupted comparison

READ FIRST: EZEKIEL 28:12–17

When our spirits are isolated, we adopt the internal posture of a spiritual orphan – alone, abandoned, afraid. In the scripture you have just read from Ezekiel 28, we see Satan, the ultimate orphaned spirit, being cast from God's presence because of his conceit and ambition.

Conceit and ambition are two of the most common manifestations in us too when we operate from an orphaned posture. They are what results when corrupted thinking intersects with God's perfect design. Woven into us as human beings are certain qualities which, if surrendered to and fuelled by God, are powerful to advance His kingdom and bring us significance. But when they are corrupted by the same comparison-based pride that drove Satan, they bring about a slow destruction of our souls.

This is a destruction God dearly wants to reverse.

Let's look first at conceit. Within God's design of us as people is the wonderful need to operate within community. We are at our best when we are found within a web of relationships that complement our strengths and compensate for weakness.

One of the most powerful facets of these relationships is their potential to reflect the heart of God in drawing people towards their destiny. We are to draw out the gold in each other, seeing potential, then investing in and encouraging it. When people speak into our lives this way we come alive spiritually. We are designed to ingest a certain amount of validation and security from the value placed on us by others. This comes initially and primarily through our parents, but as we mature we look to God and, to a much lesser degree, to others.

It is natural to conclude that we are valuable because we are valuable to them.

However, our modern societies tend to be much weaker in the area of healthy relationships than we need. And yet our hunger for validation remains, and it is at this point that the mechanism for an orphaned spirit can become our driver.

In our aloneness, we take the initiative to seek validation by means other than a healthy understanding of how God and people value us.

We often begin to compete for value with the very people who are supposed to give it.

Conceit is a slave driver that never tires. It is based in a repeated sideways glance that compares our looks, abilities and achievements to those around us. If we do well, we feel temporarily good about ourselves, or at least not as bad as we would if we fell short.

At its worst, people will do almost anything in the quest to appear perfect – cosmetic surgery, photo-shopped images, addiction to brands, excessive mortgages on impressive property, starvation, anything that makes them appear on top or at worst keeping up.

Read again the core of Satan's fall:

> *"Your heart became proud on account of your beauty, and you corrupted your wisdom because of your splendour".* (Ezekiel 28:17)

Wisdom was corrupted by comparison and conceit, and the same debilitating sadness awaits all who rely on validation apart from God's ordained design. Ultimately it is He who determines our value, and that has been shouted from the heavens by His preparedness to die for us. He values us that much.

If we cannot grasp and accept the value God places on us, we might spend a lifetime pursuing validation from conceit. And conceit's partner is ambition.

Ambition is a corrupted version of the valid tension God wove into humanity that longs to see things progress.

I say it is a tension because a redeemed desire for progress is also able to exist in the presence of sameness. In God's design we can be at peace with a degree of consistency while also enjoying the challenge of advancing our situation. God put this tension in us so that we would take the initiative to spread the influence of His kingdom beyond the walls of the comfort of Eden. As those who inherited something of the creative nature of God, longing to convert disorder into order, we were free to invent, create and expand.

Ambition, however, is a self-focused and self-promoting drive to advance in order to find an increased sense of significance.

It takes a godly hunger for development and corrupts it into a desperation for more. The absence of progress actually starves an ambitious heart, and they simply have to do better to find temporary peace. Like conceit, it is a compulsion that is never fully satisfied and is, therefore, a cruel slave driver.

For many, conceit and ambition first appear to fill the vacuum left by conditionally supportive parents or a culture that sends repeated messages about the value of high performance. We might be eight years old when we first do well in a sporting event or put on a pretty dress that attracts attention. The message is clear because it might be the only time we get it …"Great job son, you won!" or "You were more beautiful than all the others, dear".

However it might begin, the progression is predictable. Once we find a way to win at something, we long again for the high we get from either the accolades of others or the internal satisfaction that comes from rising above the pack. This replaces the normal developing mechanism of healthy self-talk and relationships which provide value in who we are regardless of performance.

It can be a significant challenge to unravel the ball of string which is a personality based in conceit and ambition. What happens when a person who has developed their whole inner world around the high of a "win" is suddenly confronted with the fact that their worth is built on a lie? What is left when you strip away a whole personality built on supposed success?

That is why God does this process slowly, allowing a person to reconstruct piece by piece the foundation of their worth by applying God's truth to their inner desperation. The truth is that we are valuable despite our performance – we are significant as we are, without trying to earn it. Ultimately, the solution to conceit and ambition is found in reversing their cause – rather than having our needs met apart from God, we are to have them met in deep relationship with Him.

Most of our issues are rooted in our separation from God, and all of our issues are resolved by finding ourselves in Him.

PRAYER

Lord, where have I tried to replace your acceptance with my own performance?

Are there needs that I am allowing to be met through comparison, which are supposed to be met through you? Show me who I truly am in your sight. Fill me again with your Spirit of adoption.

Amen

YOUR RESPONSE

How does conceit manifest in your life?

_____

_____

_____

_____

_____

How would you describe your level of ambition to do better in life?

_____

_____

_____

_____

_____

_____

What do you think is driving these issues in you?

_____

_____

_____

_____

_____

_____

1.6

Redeemed hope

The passage from Colossians 3:1–17 presents us with a wonderful contrast between two types of thinking. Paul exhorts the readers to fix their hearts on the qualities of heaven and reject the corrupted thinking of the old life. To fix our hearts means we think on those things, but it also adds an element of longing. We are to actually yearn deeply for the facets of kingdom life like kindness, humility and forgiveness.

This yearning is based in what the Bible calls hope.

Hope is a way of thinking that looks to what can and should be, and excitedly invites that future reality in our present situation. However, there is nothing whimsical in this form of hope. Paul starts the Colossians 3 passage by stating that we are already seated with Christ in a positional sense. That means our official residency is already in heaven, even though we currently live on earth.

And just as a nation's ambassador who takes up residence in a foreign land has privileged access, we too can draw from the authority and benefits of our own nation. We can actually bring the reality of our permanent home into our temporal home. That is why Jesus gave us permission to pray, *"May your will be done on earth as it is in heaven"*.

We have permission to constantly hope that our present life and circumstance will look more and more like our future.

The implications for this on our current culture are huge.

We live in a time that seems bereft of hope. In an era where there are more readily available pleasures and forms of entertainment than the world has ever seen, we also see the highest rates of depression, anxiety, suicide and profound hopelessness.

That's because many have so little to live for, so little hope that their life will improve, and so little faith in their own ability to endure that!

Proverbs 13:12 tells us that *"Hope deferred makes the heart sick, but a longing fulfilled is a tree of life"*.

Amazingly, however, during our planet's darkest hours such as the World Wars and Great Depression, people displayed massive quantities of resilience and optimism.

They longed for and believed in a preferred future and dug deep to ensure they kept on that path.

Hope, particularly well-founded hope, provides a steady compass towards a longing fulfilled. It keeps us planning for better, praying for heaven's blessings on those we love, and rejoicing in the smallest of signs of progress.

As Hebrews 6:19 says, *"We have this hope as an anchor for the soul, firm and secure"*. Hope keeps our souls steady, preventing us from sinking. It keeps us afloat through life's storms, ensuring we keep our eyes on what can and will be, not on the inevitability of disappointment. Indeed, to lose hope in any situation is actually to be under the influence of a lie that says God and His provision is not within reach.

Hopelessness is somewhat inevitable in those who are separated from Christ, since he is our only valid source of hope. An orphaned spirit is constantly reminded of the limitations of their own resources and the uncertainty of the future. After all, what future is there without Christ?

When we are separate from Christ, our logic is defiled by the inadequacy of our own strength. We logically look to our past as the projector of our future, knowing that the failures of yesterday can only be replicated tomorrow – since I know I will be the same person then as I am now.

The spiritual person (the *pneumatikos*), however, is not constrained by who they were yesterday. In fact, the failures and wounds from the past are the one thing we have no claim to at all!

Our eternity is based on who Christ is in us! He determines the shape of tomorrow. It is God who speaks in to who I can be, and gives me the strength to fulfil it. Look at how Paul describes us in 1 Corinthians 3:21–23, *"All things are yours, whether Paul or Apollos or Cephas or the world or life or death or the present or the future—all are yours, and you are of Christ, and Christ is of God"*.

Notice that he said the present and future are ours, but Paul makes no mention of yesterday. That is because God owns your yesterday and has declared it of no consequence for your future. That means your weaknesses, your wounds, your mistakes and your limitations are no longer your reckoning point.

God only calls us forward, assuming we are unshackled from the past. He calls us by a name that depicts what we can be and should be. It is a name rooted in Christian hope.

And yet it is not only possible, but actually inevitable, that without learning how to be in powerful partnership with God's Spirit we live as if our shackles are still in place. Those who are without hope can only remain so if they reason as they did before they met Christ.

This is why Paul made such a foundational and repeated point that *"Since you have been raised with Christ, set your hearts on things above, where Christ is, seated at the right hand of God.*

Set your minds on things above, not on earthly things" (Colossians 3:1-2).

Your destiny relies on *pneuma* (God's breath) being your life source.

Whenever you live apart from God, you choose a lesser path. One without a preferred future and one with very little hope. It is the path of the orphan – alone, afraid, locked down in sin, having to compete for significance and ultimately remaining fruitless.

Jesus offers you a preferred future full of hope and fruit. But He prefaced that by saying in John 15:5 that *"I am the vine; you are the branches. If you remain in me and I in you, you will bear much fruit; apart from me you can do nothing"*.

It can't be any clearer, can it?

Every problem in humanity has its roots in us living in separation from God. But every hope, every solution, every transformation, every ounce of worthy potential is found in returning to deep union with Christ.

This is your redeemed hope – anything less is at best a half-life of dust without breath.

Prayer

Lord, help me today to place my hope in you. Where I place my hope in circumstance or people, help me to focus instead on you to meet my deepest needs.

In you, LORD my God, I put my trust. I trust in you; do not let me be put to shame, nor let my enemies triumph over me. No one who hopes in you will ever be put to shame, but shame will come on those who are treacherous without cause. Show me your ways, LORD, teach me your paths. Guide me in your truth and teach me, for you are God my Savior, and my hope is in you all day long. (Psalm 25:1–5)

Amen

Your response

Considering the various slave drivers and idols brought to your attention this week, how different might the future look for you if God could heal and empower you for freedom? How would you describe that freedom? Is it a future you would actually prefer?

Group Session 2

INTRODUCTION

This first group of readings (1.1 thru 1.6) shone a light on the contrasting vision that both Jesus and Satan have for your life.

Jesus offers you abundance and freedom, while Satan is intent on destroying your destiny in Christ.

> *The thief comes only to steal and kill and destroy;*
> *I have come that they may have life,*
> *and have it to the full.* (John **10:10**)

Q. What was your overall response to the material this week?

_____

_____

_____

Your responses from the past week

God is calling you to experience a unique form of abundant life – one with fruit based on the name He has for us in heaven. Share together your responses from chapters 1.1 and 1.2.

> **1.1** What is your response to this offer of life? Is this what you want? Do you yearn for relief from the agendas of this world and the need to do well or look good? Spend a few minutes writing down your response and desire for God at the beginning of this course. At the end, things may well look very different for you.

> **1.2** What has God been dealing with in your life? Does any area continually come up as a problem? If you had to guess, what do you think you need to put to death so you can fully live?

TO WALK IN FREEDOM, WE MUST IDENTIFY AND BREAK THAT WHICH CONSTRAINS US.

The seed that fell among thorns stands for those who hear, but as they go on their way they are choked by life's worries, riches and pleasures, and they do not mature. (Luke 8:14)

Share together your responses from chapters 1.3 thru 1.5.

1.3 (4): What is the most consistent issue you battle with in life that you know is holding you back or limiting your spiritual growth?

Is there a particular fear, addiction, relational dysfunction, shame or other consistent issue that you struggle to control?

What is it that you consistently do that you know is not God's plan for you?

1.4 What idols are present in your life?

1.5 How does conceit manifest in your life?

How would you describe your level of ambition to do better in life?

What do you think is driving these issues in you?

OUR HOPE CAN ONLY BE FOUND IN CHRIST.

We have this hope as an anchor for the soul, firm and secure. (Hebrew 6:19)

Share now your hopes for overcoming from your response to chapter 1.6.

1.6 Considering the various slave drivers and idols brought to your attention this week, how different might the future look for you if God could heal and empower you for freedom? How would you describe that freedom? Is it a future you would actually prefer?

In closing, pray for each other that Christ would give them clarity in their hopes and dreams. Seek God for specific grace to overcome the issues raised through this week's material.

2.1

Out of the box

After seeing Jesus walk on water, Mark 6:51 tells us that the disciples were completely amazed. You might think that unsurprising – after all, no one had walked on water before!

The writer, however, gives us the impression that their amazement was not the right response. *"They were completely amazed, for they had not understood about the loaves; their hearts were hardened"*.

Earlier that day Jesus had miraculously fed the five thousand, and it apparently should have opened their hearts. They were supposed to be beyond amazement now. Their thinking was meant to be out of the box for good.

What box might that be?

The box is the constrained way that we think. It is logic that begins with what we know, and builds a case for the future on the accumulated wisdom and experience of the past. We tend to look at what is in our box for the tools to build our next step in life.

The box relies on us. Our own strength is the limit and our own ideas define what is possible.

After their abject lesson on the lake, the disciples were given another chance to get out of the box. Mark 8 describes Jesus doing the same thing again, this time feeding four thousand people with only seven loaves. Then Jesus, being somewhat frustrated with the religious and unbelieving mindsets of the Pharisees, got back in the boat with the disciples.

They had forgotten their own lunch, however, and sat staring at their single loaf, wondering who would miss out.

"Why are you talking about having no bread", Jesus said. *"Do you still not see or understand? Are your hearts hardened?"*[1]

The miracles were supposed to recalibrate their thinking. The low-water mark for their faith was meant to be what Jesus had just demonstrated. The same goes for us.

Has God ever done anything miraculous in you? Have you heard testimony of what He has done in others? These examples of reality give you permission to think out of your box.

Hopelessness is rooted in a mindset that says, *"What will be is up to me"*. Hope is rooted in the mindset that says, *"Anything is possible because God is helping, and I have permission to go for whatever Jesus would go for"*.

Jesus clearly promised that we would do greater things than He has done[2]. And this has all sorts of implications for you.

You may remember from the previous chapter that your past, with all its failures, hurts and weakness, belongs hidden with God. You have permission to look forward with eyes wide open, expectant that God is with you making all things possible.

Yet one of the least common things for 21st century believers to do is form a picture of what they want to aim for in Christ. We have dreams for our finance, pathways for our career, we even plan for our future holidays. And yet we struggle to dream of what God might do in us.

Perhaps it stems from the challenges of collaboration? It is simpler to make up our own mind of what should be done, restricting our plan to the limitations of our own strength and discipline. Negotiating with a second party makes things complex, especially since any partnership with God is bound to be an unbalanced and potentially unpredictable one!

So, we instead keep our dreams simple, small and somewhat safe.

I am convinced that one of the reasons we do not hear all that God is saying to us is that our ears are not tuned to hear His language of hope. He is continually inviting us into the seemingly impossible. Since He has no limit, His plans for us take the same form.

When we come to dialogue with Him, we might begin with phrases like this: *"God, it is impossible"*, or *"I am hopeless"*, or *"I cannot possibly endure this"*. And we wonder why He seems absent at that point. But He is not absent, He simply is not entering in to a conversation that He fundamentally disagrees with.

We need to change the conversation if we want Him to join in! We might need to ask Him about how to partner with His promised help. We may need to seek Him for possibilities we haven't thought of. We can definitely look for ways in which to bring Him glory, no matter what is going on. These are topics God loves to engage in because they line up with His thinking.

The starting point for our logic is what God has said and done. Ephesians 3:20 says that He is able to do more than we can ask or imagine, according to His power at work within us. Note that it is His power in you which is the key. It is not a power that is remote from you. We are not to be passive, sitting back uninvolved or unaccountable.

The way we think and act matters. Our ability to grow our hope-oriented partnership with God is the key to so many New Testament promises that, for many, remain unattainable.

Your failures, your addictions, your insecurity and fears ... all of them need to bow to the reality of the sufficiency of Christ in you. The determinant of your future direction is found in one simple verse from Colossians 1:27, *"Christ in you the hope of glory"*.

Your past limitations are a box – one that is too small for God, let alone you. It is time to get out of it!

Christ in you is powerful and He wants to be let out! He wants to start with the hopes of your God-given imagination and then burst beyond them.

It starts with a dream; a desire for life to look somewhat different. We need to grow our skill at forming a preferred future for ourselves that does not anchor itself to our past. No decision for your future, if based in yesterday's fear, is the right one. No dream for impact in the world, if it allows you to harbour the hurts of the past, is going to be the shape and size of God's dream.

It is time for you to dream with God. Most of what Jesus did that amazed those around Him had no precedent. Feeding thousands and walking on water was all new. What new thing might He want to do in you?

Prayer

Father, what box have I allowed life to put me in?

What judgments of me have I believed and what lies about myself have I told? I choose to agree with your truth today, that you are indeed my hope of glory.

Amen

References

1. Mark 8:17
2. John 14:12

Your response

Is there an area of your life where you have lost hope? You can tell, because it will be an area where you don't plan to see change happen. Perhaps it is as little as a way of thinking, or as large as your hopes for calling, happiness and legacy. Where do you find it hardest to hope?

_____

_____

_____

_____

_____

_____

_____

_____

_____

_____

_____

_____

_____

_____

_____

_____

_____

_____

_____

_____

_____

_____

2.2

The posture of hope

READ FIRST: LUKE 18:9–14

The Pharisees of Jesus' day formed their view of righteousness in a comparative way. They would strive to do their best at adhering to the meticulous and outward regulations of Moses' Law and compare themselves with others.

The main point was not that they were perfect but that they could regard themselves as more righteous than anyone else, and thus be more deserving of God's favour. They measured sinlessness from the height of their own eye level. As such, their spiritual posture was as straight and rigid as possible.

Jesus called them stiff-necked – unwilling to turn. And yet life with God is all about turning. We are to turn towards Him in worship, and also turn towards Him in repentance.

2 Corinthians 3:15–16 says that *"Even to this day when Moses is read, a veil covers their hearts. But whenever anyone turns to the Lord, the veil is taken away"*.

The Pharisee in today's reading from Luke 18 was veiled from God's presence, even though he stood in God's very temple praying. His posture kept Him from receiving God's grace, while the one he looked down on was forgiven. In comparing, the Pharisee remained but dust.

The beggar, on the other hand, had a posture that received. He was wanting to receive grace, ready to turn, and desiring God's forgiveness.

These two postures exemplify the difference between those who receive from God and those who don't. Those who desire Him, regardless of their performance, history or relative standard, will find Him.

The Pharisee was described by Jesus as one who stood by himself. This is the problem; we are not designed to stand by ourselves. We are dust and breath, relegated to living a half-life if we are alone. Our perceived standard is completely irrelevant – before God we all look much the same on the righteousness scale.

What gets His attention is sincere hunger.

God wants to engage with those who desire Him. We are in a relationship after all, not a business contract! We are not slaves who need to please a master. Jesus called us friends and brothers[1]. Paul described us as sons, those adored by the Father and released to grow the family inheritance[2].

James 4:8 tells us to *"draw near to God, and He will draw near to us"*. There is a need for genuine and consistent intent on our part. Because our engagement with God is relational and our human fulfilment is found in intimacy, we are to pursue Him sincerely.

Prayers are not answered just because we finish with *"in Jesus' name"*. God does not respond to formulas or presumptive mantras. He engages with us personally – heart to heart. Psalm 42:7 declares that *"Deep calls to deep in the roar of your waterfalls; all your waves and breakers have swept over me"*.

The Psalmist is talking there about an intense, emotional and spiritual experience of God. It is an experience that must be sought after, not waited for passively and stiffly.

The language of hope is desire.

If you hope to change your life, overcome sin, breakthrough in your calling, or even love people more, then you need to genuinely want it!

I do not mean here that you would merely take it if it was offered, reaching out to grasp something that is handed to you. I am referring to a form of desire that motivates you to do something.

Hebrews 11:6 says that God rewards those who earnestly seek Him. The original Greek wording there refers to a desire that is hand-cuffed to an intent. It infers that you cannot genuinely desire something if you aren't pursuing it.

And so we might define three categories of posture in regard to hope – the Unwilling, the Willing, and a third category we called the Wanting.

The Unwilling category is illustrated by the Pharisee in Jesus' story from Luke 18. They are rigid, unwilling to consider change and somewhat self-righteous in their stance. Because they do not want to change, they never will. A believer can go through decades of exposure to teaching and trial and still never grow. Growth is not a function of time but of desire.

The category we call the Willing are those who would accept change if it were offered, but do not make an effort to initiate it. They are the passive believers who say that if God wants to do something in them then He knows their number. They are available to receive but not hungry for it.

The interesting thing about those in this second category is that throughout their life they may well receive grace from God to help them grow or progress. And yet they usually do not stay changed! Their transformation slips away because they do not know how to partner with it. They have not developed the spiritual muscles required to press in to God and access that which is only available through intimacy.

The only people who change and stay changed are those in the Wanting category.

The level of desire we exercise in any area of our spiritual life will have a huge impact on what happens next. I hesitate to add that our level of "acceptable desire" and God's are starkly different. In Jeremiah 29:13 God says that *"You will seek me and find me when you seek me with all your heart"*.

This all begs the question then: How much do you desire a better outcome in your life?

Do you really long to overcome a way of thinking or behaving? Do you really want to engage more deeply with God and see His grace working powerfully in you and in your world? If your desire is low, then perhaps your first dream should be to grow your desire!

The truth is, your spiritual life is exactly where you want it. God will not create desire in you, it is yours to create and pursue. That is your gift and your responsibility. Today you get to choose where you will focus and grow your desire.

PRAYER

Pray the sections of this Psalm to God:

> *(You) The LORD are my light and my*
> *salvation—whom shall I fear?*

> *You are the stronghold of my life—*
> *of whom shall I be afraid?*

When the wicked advance against me to devour me, it is my enemies and my foes who will stumble and fall. Though an army besiege me, my heart will not fear; though war break out against me, even then I will be confident.

One thing I ask from the LORD, this only do I seek: that I may dwell in the house of the LORD all the days of my life, to gaze on the beauty of the LORD and to seek him in his temple.

For in the day of trouble he will keep me safe in his dwelling; he will hide me in the shelter of his sacred tent and set me high upon a rock. Then my head will be exalted above the enemies who surround me; at his sacred tent I will sacrifice with shouts of joy; I will sing and make music to the LORD. Hear my voice when I call, LORD; be merciful to me and answer me.

My heart says of you, "Seek his face!"
Your face, LORD, I will seek.

I remain confident of this: I will see the goodness of the LORD in the land of the living. Wait for the LORD; be strong and take heart and wait for the LORD. (Psalm 27:1–14)

REFERENCES

1. Mark 3:34; John 15:5
2. Romans 8:14–16; Galatians 4:6

YOUR RESPONSE

How would you describe your level of desire for change or a better future? If you had to rate it on a scale, where is it currently and where do you believe it should be?

_____

_____

_____

_____

_____

_____

_____

_____

_____

_____

_____

_____

2.3

Building desire

An old story goes that a grandfather was explaining to his grandson that there are two wolves within all of us. One of them is a good wolf which represents kindness, courage, love and all the things we would prefer to be. The bad wolf represents all our negative drivers and desires like fear, rage and bitterness.

The grandson thinks about this for a moment, then looks up and asks, *"Which one wins, Pop?"* The old man quietly replies, *"The one you feed"*.

It may surprise you, but desire is something we can create and grow. The presence or absence of desire does not represent inevitability. Like a physical hunger, we can change what we desire by regularly investing in it. Any elite sportsman will confirm that their motivation is something to be intentionally developed lest their performance suffer.

We are to be developers of desire, not victims of it. We get to choose and grow where our desires are focused.

Some naïvely use desire as their primary guide. They follow a certain life path, or pursue an obsession based on the assumption that their passions are a God-given green light.

We should, however, see our desires as a wake, not a rudder. Passions should not determine your direction; they follow your commitment to it.

As you read Romans seven and eight, Paul describes the "two wolves" of our inner world. One is our old nature which, although rendered powerless by the presence of God's Spirit within, can still function if we invest in it. The other is our new nature, controlled by the Spirit of God.

It is this new nature that Paul says we are now obliged to follow. We may feel obliged to sin, and we may even desire to follow that old nature, but we are not as obligated as we feel.

This book is all about giving you the formational tools to become the *pneumatikos*, the spiritual person mentioned in 1 Corinthians 3:1. The scriptures teach us that the Spirit in our life bears fruit such as love, peace, joy, patience and more[1].

In Romans 8, Paul says that it is the presence of God's Spirit which is the circuit breaker in determining which wolf we feed. In the absence of the Spirit we have no choice but to feed our old, broken selves. Our desires follow our investment in that side of our life.

But you are a Christian! In Galatians 5 Paul first describes the fruit of the Spirit then says clearly that *"Those who belong to Christ have crucified the flesh with its passions and desires"*[2].

Did you get that? He says we *have* crucified those desires – past tense. They are history.

They may, like the proverbial zombie, raise their head and cry out to be fed. But make no mistake, you are not obliged to follow, and they will fade. God's Spirit has all the power you need to turn in a better direction but you need to want that turn.

That is where desire comes in. Desire follows commitment, and energy follows intention. Once we commit to and start making steps to follow a preferred future, our enthusiasm for that gains momentum and strength.

Desire is a powerful thing. It drives so many of our decisions and habits. It compels a man to pursue a woman, even if she shows no interest. It motivates sportspeople to endure incredible pain and continual sacrifice. It fuels the heart of a mother to sacrifice for her young children, even after endless days of crying or even unrequited affection.

Those desires are birthed in something deeper than an emotion.

Desire is a by-product of value. What we value will drive our commitments, and what we commit to drives our desire.

Jesus put it this way, *"Where your treasure is, there your heart will be also"*[3].

Whatever it is that you truly hold dear will be the direction of your passion. To build the right desire, we need to remind ourselves of what is truly important on a regular basis. When forming a picture of a preferred future, we need to ensure it is built on what we know we are prepared to fight for.

We must also ensure that our way of getting to that future also meets our values. The ends do not justify any means. In fact, it is the journey itself that fuels our heart, not arriving at the future destination. And so we must form ourselves a picture of how to live, not of how to arrive.

King David had to get this issue squared away very early in his journey to fulfilling his dream. At age 16 he had been promised the kingdom of Israel, but in short order the existing king, Saul, had David exiled. Saul then went further, pursuing David with the aim of killing him.

David was guiltless and could have found many ways to get to His promised future, but his core values drove the way that journey was fulfilled. That way he could find peace and joy on the whole path rather than storing up his happiness for a future that often looked uncertain.

One day Saul stumbled into a dark cave in which David and his men were hiding. They encouraged David to end it all right there, killing the defenceless and unworthy king and taking up his mantle. But David had a core value of honour and submission that would not let him harm his ruler[4].

For David it was unthinkable to gain his preferred future if he lost his integrity in the process. It has been said, *"You may win the rat-race, but you are still a rat"*, but that was not how David would live.

He expressed his heart of desire often in the Psalms. There we get insight into the things that really mattered to this man under intense pressure. *"My soul yearns, even faints, for the courts of the Lord; my heart and my flesh cry out for the living God"*[5].

That is desire speaking. David's intensity and passion came from his deeply held belief that God and His causes were more valuable than anything else. These beliefs were his guiding compass. They had been formed from years in the fields guarding sheep and worshipping God. His beliefs fuelled his passion.

In other Psalms David would vent his other, less-optimistic emotions. His frustration at injustice, his desire for his enemies to be slaughtered and judged, his regret for sins committed. Usually, however, he would shake himself free of the pain and remember his God, and the reasons for his journey.

Do you know your reasons? Have you defined the things that matter to you? Your desires are coming from somewhere, and in the absence of a worthy cause, the black wolf waits for any emotional food that isn't put to good use. You get to decide which passions get fed.

PRAYER

Father, when I understand the elements of desire, I want my heart to desire only you.

Forgive me when my heart has wandered and my passions have been off track. Draw me back to you and the things of value in your courts. Bring the best of my passions back towards you.

Amen

REFERENCES

1. Galatians 5:22–23
2. Galatians 5:24
3. Matthew 6:21
4. 1 Samuel 24
5. Psalm 84:2

YOUR RESPONSE

The Psalms are full of David's prayers and desires. If you were to write a note like that to God, what would it be? What are your desires, both good and bad? Spend a few minutes expressing your heart to God about the things that drive so much of your life right now.

_____

_____

_____

_____

_____

_____

_____

_____

_____

_____

_____

_____

_____

_____

_____

_____

2.4

Desiring God

READ FIRST: PSALM 27

Did you realise that it is possible to objectify God?

To objectify someone is to degrade their status to that of a non-personal object. It means you don't actually invest or value the relationship; you value what the person has for you or does for you.

It may surprise you to know that Christians do that to God all the time.

We come to Him in prayer with a list of things we need done ... a healing, a provision, a solution ... the bottom line is that we want Him to fix things. But often we do not want Him personally, just what He provides us.

At times we revert to engaging with Him through formulas and predictable routines. We assume that if we pray a certain way, call on a certain part of His nature, or do whatever else we think He requires then our efforts will compel Him to respond.

It sounds a little stark when I put it that way, doesn't it?

But this is why generations and cultures have so often reverted to idols. They are predictable, defined, and simple in operation. The premise is that if you pay the appropriate sacrifice then the god behind the idol will respond. There is no deep interaction involved.

Whether we follow the true God or not, the scriptures declare that all humanity has a sense of the eternal woven into us. Thus, we will constantly revert to a search for meaning and some form of divine intervention. Ecclesiastes 3:11 says that *"God has set eternity in the human heart"*. In the absence of relationship with God, fallen humanity will worship idols. They find this strangely natural because, ultimately, idols are gods created in our own image.

A study of how early tribes developed reveals how the process commonly evolves. First, a group or tribe will look for ways to define and explain themselves. They want to identify the "spirit" of the group that encapsulates their general culture, value, and even their trajectory and purpose. Often this spirit is associated with an object or animal that might represent them. It may be a lion, or an eagle or, in the case of the Hebrews leaving Egypt, a bull[1].

They then make representations of this spirit in a physical form such as a totem or statue and keep it in the middle of the tribe or place of worship. In essence, they are bowing to an idol that represents, or is "made in the image" of, the people themselves.

This is a complete inversion of the reality that it is us who reflect the image of God. We are made in His image, bearing facets of His nature in limited form. Idols represent facets of our already tarnished image, and only that in a tainted way.

This may explain why God gave the commandments in the order they came: First, *"You shall have no gods before me"*, and second, *"You shall not make for yourself an image in the form of anything in heaven"*[2]. In other words, *"No idols!"*

We are made to reflect God, not the other way around. God does not conform to our formulas and rituals; He wants to engage with you personally – Father to son, friend to friend[3].

Just look at how this played out in the life of David. He had known constant trial, rejection, slander, mortal danger and delayed promises. If anyone would benefit from an easing of circumstance, it was him. And yet his prayers are those of a person who sought God personally, not a remote deity that offered respite.

The LORD is my light and my salvation—whom shall I fear?

*… Though an army besiege me, my heart
will not fear; though war break out against
me, even then I will be confident.*

*One thing I ask from the LORD, this only do I
seek: that I may dwell in the house of the LORD
all the days of my life, to gaze on the beauty of
the LORD and to seek him in his temple.*

*My heart says of you, "Seek his face!" Your face, LORD, I
will seek.*
(Psalm 27:1–4; 8)

God described David as a man after His own heart[4]. He was one who sought God for His own sake. When he was with God, David was home.

In the last few chapters we have been considering desire. What is it you want? What do you seek for your life? What is it that you should seek, and what is worth going through an element of change for?

The desire to grow more like Christ, or even to fulfil a worthier life, must be the result of a more foundational desire – that of desiring God Himself. Without a desire to be with Him, and to love Him without agenda or hidden motive, we are potentially adding an element of objectification to the relationship.

When we desire God personally, our own agendas and wish lists change. We don't plead so much for Him to bless our situation or change our world; instead we ask Him to change us, or to reveal what His plan might be so we can join it. When thinking of a preferred future in which we focus our hopes, we will be much more fruitful if it is a life of intimacy and fruit that we seek.

We cannot simply give a nod of the head to this principle. Jesus said that a genuine and consuming love for God is the highest priority in our life[5]. It takes intention and consistency, a real determination with the best of what we have to get to know God better.

God's plans for us – the plans and hopes worth pursuing – only come into view when our focus is on Him. Listen to what God Himself says in this regard in Jeremiah 29:11–13:

> *For I know the plans I have for you," declares the LORD, "plans to prosper you and not to harm you, plans to give you hope and a future. Then you will call on me and come and pray to me, and I will listen to you.*
>
> *You will seek me and find me when you seek me with all your heart.*

It was intimate relationship with God that was lost at the fall. It is intimate relationship that was made possible again by the cross. And all that God has available for us is found by activating that relationship sincerely and passionately. God alone is to be your desire.

PRAYER

Pray this Psalm

> *You, God, are my God, earnestly I seek you; I thirst for you, my whole being longs for you, in a dry and parched land where there is no water.*

> *I have seen you in the sanctuary and beheld your power and your glory. Because your love is better than life, my lips will glorify you. I will praise you as long as I live, and in your name I will lift up my hands.*

> *I will be fully satisfied as with the richest of foods; with singing lips my mouth will praise you. On my bed I remember you; I think of you through the watches of the night. Because you are my help, I sing in the shadow of your wings.* (Psalm 63:1-7)

REFERENCES

1. Exodus 32:1–4
2. Exodus 20:3–4
3. John 15:15; Galatians 4:6–7
4. 1 Samuel 13:14
5. Matthew 22:37

YOUR RESPONSE

Consider for a moment the things you pray about – that list you bring to God for Him to address. Could it be that you have looked to Him as the giver of answers more than the lover of your soul? How might you have objectified God?

_____

_____

_____

_____

_____

_____

_____

_____

_____

_____

_____

_____

2.5

Desiring freedom

READ FIRST: 2 CORINTHIANS 3

"I wish I could just _____ "

You fill in the blank. What have you wished you could do or be differently?

If nothing comes to mind, think of a day when you were at the end of yourself. Remember a moment when you were frustrated at your performance or your life. Reflect on the disappointment of having tried to do something right or good but having failed yet again.

At those moments your self-worth takes a hit, your goals are recalibrated, and your belief in a better outcome fades away. Recognising your lack of the right stuff you say "*I wish I could just ...*"

I know. Everyone knows.

You just wanted things to be better. You wanted *you* to be better!

But, without help, you aren't better. You have shown what you've got, and it isn't enough. Not yet anyway. Not without some added element coming in to the equation.

This is the story of all of us without the personal and ongoing help of God. We are not free! We are bound up in every limitation of sin, unable to get past those things that keep us down. When sin controls our life, we are like slaves deprived of choice. We feel compelled to obey, chained to thinking and behaviour, suffering a slow death of a thousand cuts[1].

But our reading from 2 Corinthians 3 draws a stark contrast between this debilitating decline and the offer of the Spirit saying, *"Where the Spirit of the Lord is, there is freedom"*[2].

What is this freedom? How does it work? What can I do to attain this offer, which scripture repeats time and again?

It would seem from the preceding verse that it's all in the *turn*. Paul says that *"Whenever anyone turns to the Lord, the veil is taken away"*[3].

To turn to the Lord means I turn away from relying on my own strength and rely on what He has done for me at the cross. At the cross I gained unfettered access to God, demonstrated by the presence and power of the Holy Spirit in me[4]. And as we have read, His Spirit is the promise of freedom!

Is freedom what you want?

As I have walked with thousands on this journey of transformation, the most common blockage seen is not the magnitude of sin or wounding but the smallness of people's desire to change. Most of us have become so used to our spiritual level – so familiar with our habits and limitations – that the pain of staying the same seems more attractive than the pain of change.

That is, until they form a genuinely preferred future, or know what it is like to experience a degree of freedom.

Perhaps I can illustrate it this way. Like many people these days, I have taken up cycling as a way to stay fit and escape the rigours of the office. Being a semi-obsessive type, I became a little enamoured with increasing my fitness and speed. Eventually I reached the level that my available hours permitted and found a degree of harmony between health, muscle strength and actual aerobic fitness.

At one point my travel schedule required me to have a couple of months off the bike. When I eventually hit the training hills again to get some speed back, I thought it would be my legs that would hurt the most, but the pain came from my lungs!

I just couldn't seem to breathe. At least not enough to provide oxygen and blood to my muscles which seemed under no load at all. I had to force myself to exert less effort, even though I didn't seem to be working that hard. The fact was, I had to reduce my expectations back to the capacity of my breathing.

This is what we do with our spiritual life as well.

We might try living up to the standards of scripture, giving it focused effort. But eventually the limitations of our own strength are displayed through repeated failure, and so we reset our expectations.

What we have in fact done is adjust our life and dreams to the level of our spiritual breathing.

With my cycling, however, I had in the past seen a better day. I had experienced better performance and knew I could get here again. It was a preferred future that I desired to see again. I just had to grow my capacity to breathe.

How do we do that? By turning to God.

Much of the remainder of this book will show you some exciting facets of how to do that. But the first and most powerful one is seen in the final verse of 2 Corinthians 3:

> *And we all, who with unveiled faces contemplate*
> *the Lord's glory, are being transformed into*

*his image with ever-increasing glory, which
comes from the Lord, who is the Spirit.*

As we turn to Him, we begin to gaze on Him. Then, as we continue to contemplate His glory, we are somehow transformed to be more like the One we adore.

It is normal to reflect the traits of the one you worship or admire, but there is an extra dynamic that comes in to play as we fix our eyes on Christ. That dynamic is one of empowered alignment.

As we come in to line with His will in our hearts, and follow on with action, the Spirit empowers that choice, giving us the ability to fulfil it.

We are beginning to breathe! And that breathing becomes addictive. The more you do it, the more you want it.

This then becomes our desire – more freedom! You want to unclog your spiritual lungs more and more. Your once habitual sin begins to look unattractive as you realise how it damages the intimacy you long for.

For some it is this simple. They desire Christ and turn away from all else to gaze on Him alone. Their freedom comes naturally. For others it is a longer journey. But the desire for freedom ensures that it is indeed freedom that is found.

Have you settled for less than the freedom Christ offers you? Perhaps it is time to reshape your preferred future and desire that which the Spirit desires for you. As James 4:5 says:

> *Do you think Scripture says in vain, "The Spirit who dwells in us yearns jealously?*

PRAYER

My true freedom is found in you, God. I repent of living for you in the absence of living from you. Help me to breathe.

Help me yearn for you with a glimmer of the desire with which you yearn for me. Show me today when I need to breathe in your grace more and more. Show me what is clogging my spiritual lungs.

Amen

REFERENCES

1. Romans 6:16
2. 2 Corinthians 3:17
3. 2 Corinthians 3:16
4. 2 Corinthians 1:22
5. 2 Corinthians 3:18

YOUR RESPONSE

What is clogging your spiritual lungs? Is there a sin you feel obliged to, or a bitterness that you can't let go of? Perhaps you are afraid, or addicted to control or comfort or pleasure. Ask God to reveal to you what is clogging your spiritual lungs.

_____

_____

_____

_____

_____

_____

_____

_____

_____

_____

_____

_____

_____

_____

_____

2.6

Creating a hope

READ FIRST: 1 KINGS 8:14–18

As Solomon stood before all the elders and people of Israel to dedicate the temple he had finally completed, he was in the shadow of his father David.

Even though Solomon had paid for and organised the work, David had inspired and planned it. It was David's dream to build a place that reflected the greatness of God in some symbolic way. He wanted people to see the building and be awestruck. He wanted God to dwell in a place befitting His majesty, if only that was possible.

The temple wasn't God's idea. In fact, God was happy to dwell in a tent that could be moved around. And yet God was pleased to see the temple built. Not for His sake, but for the sake of David.

Since the day I brought my people Israel out of Egypt,
I have not chosen a city in any tribe of Israel to have
a temple built so that my Name might be there, but
I have chosen David to rule my people Israel.[1]

God didn't choose a temple; He chose a person.

But that person had in mind a better future, one where God was glorified fully by His people. God loves it when we dream of better things, especially those things which fulfil our design and calling. He doesn't always tell us what to do because he treats us as His children, not slaves.

He loves it when we imagine. He wired us for hope and knows that when we dream we are doing what our minds were made for. As soon as David had time to think of something besides ridding Israel of God's enemies, his thoughts turned to another worthy purpose.

After the king was settled in his palace and the LORD
had given him rest from all his enemies around him, he
said to Nathan the prophet, "Here I am, living in a house
of cedar, while the ark of God remains in a tent."

Nathan replied to the king, "Whatever you have in
mind, go ahead and do it, for the LORD is with you."[2]

We have permission to hope for a better future, in fact, it is expected. But, like David, we need to first realise that our present reality is no longer acceptable. For David, the thought of God dwelling in a humble tent was unthinkable – it went against his core values and reverence for God.

And even though David's priorities and God's were not quite the same, still God said to him, *"You did well to have it in your heart to build a temple for my Name"*[3].

So, what about you?

Is hope woven in to your thinking? Is your present reality acceptable?

You may not dream of building a temple, but do you hope to realise more freedom and fruit than you currently do? Is there enough of God's power working through you daily? Are you at peace through the storms of your life? Are you comfortable in your own skin, or do shame and fear eat away at your inner security?

Think of the slave drivers and idols that influence much of our lives. Does comfort or materialism control you, or are you compelled to a higher calling that stretches you a little more? Is addiction your master, or is your love for God driving behaviour and thought?

What in your present life can no longer be tolerated?

Now, what would life look like if God had his way in that area? How different could it look, how much better could it be?

Remember, God is willing and able to do more than we can ask or imagine, according to His power at work in us[4]. That means that no matter how big or ambitious our plans might be, they will never out-do God's ability.

The key is that our hopes must rely on Him, not us alone.

The whole premise of this book is built on the fact that, as God calls us on, our next steps are built on a deeper partnership. A change in our life will come from a change in our relationship with God. He calls us deeper in to Him, and that changes the way our life looks externally.

God always has more. There are facets to His nature and His dealings with you that you have not experienced yet. He draws you on so you can grasp them. He is better than you think, so He wants to change the way you are thinking!

Hope does that for us, and that is why it is so vital. It forces us to look beyond the pain of the past and reconfigure our expectations based on God's goodness, not our failures.

We need to create hope by forming a picture in our mind of a preferred future, one that takes us beyond the unacceptable present.

If fear is an issue, what would it look like if that fear was gone? What would you do, how would it feel? Write it down and dwell on that potential, because God is for you, not against you[5].

If you seem to be controlled by body image, sexual addiction or restless ambition, create a picture of what it could be like if that was not the case. Then aim for that preferred future.

> *We have this hope as an anchor for*
> *the soul, firm and secure.*[6]

Anchors are secure, anchors have a rope. When we anchor our hopes in a preferred future, we can grab that rope and draw ourselves home. Without hope, we are resigned to stagnation.

The incredible thing is that David never did see the temple built. And yet he saw it fully in his mind, as if it was real. The best hopes and dreams are those that go beyond us and make a better future for others.

What is a dream worth having for you? What hope do you need as an anchor for your soul?

PRAYER

Father, please clarify my vision for a life worth living. Grant me creativity to think outside of the life I have seen so far. Show me a picture and a dream worth pursuing for a lifetime.

Amen

REFERENCES

1. 1 Kings 8:16
2. 2 Samuel 7:1-3
3. 1 Kings 8:18
4. Ephesians 3:20
5. Romans 8:31
6. Hebrews 6:19

YOUR RESPONSE

Are you able to identify your unacceptable present and your preferred future? Write them down and lay out a dream before God of a life worth fighting for.

_____

_____

_____

_____

_____

_____

_____

_____

_____

Group Session 3

INTRODUCTION

Holy desire is not a common issue to raise in Western churches. And yet it is a fundamental part of kingdom culture that we can only overlook if we are determined to.

Q. What was your over-arching response to the material this week?

YOUR RESPONSES FROM THE PAST WEEK

For many, it is confronting to realise that we need to go beyond being willing for God to change us, but actually wanting Him to. Share with each other your responses to chapters 2.1 thru 2.5.

> **2.1** Is there an area of your life where you have lost hope? You can tell, because it will be an area where you don't plan to see change happen. Perhaps it is as little as a way of thinking, or as large as your

hopes for calling, happiness and legacy. Where do you find it hardest to hope?

2.2 How would you describe your level of desire for change or a better future? If you had to rate it on a scale, where is it currently and where do you believe it should be?

2.3 The Psalms are full of David's prayers and desires. If you were to write a note like that to God, what would it be? What are your desires, both good and bad? Spend a few minutes expressing your heart to God about the things that drive so much of your life right now.

2.4 Consider for a moment the things you pray about – that list you bring to God for Him to address. Could it be that you have looked to Him as the giver of answers more than the lover of your soul? How might you have objectified God?

2.5 What is clogging your spiritual lungs? Is there a sin you feel obliged to, or a bitterness that you can't let go of? Perhaps you are afraid, or addicted to control or comfort or pleasure. Ask God to reveal to you what is clogging your spiritual lungs.

How then do your present and preferred future differ? Share your response to session 2.6.

2.6 Are you able to identify your unacceptable present and your preferred future? Write them down and lay out a dream before God of a life worth fighting for.

A PREFERRED FUTURE

What are the facets of my current reality that are unacceptable?	What might be the opposite, or preferred, alternative?

Share with each other the detail of your dream for a preferred future.

How would your feelings be different?

_____

What habits would change?

_____

What relationships might be altered, ceased or started?

_____

How would you invest you time differently?

_____

_____

_____

In closing, pray for each other that God would stir up and confirm this dream.

3.1

What time is it?

READ FIRST: PSALM 32

Life can seem to change in a moment – even if it is merely our perception that shifts.

At first the outlook might be grim and the weight of our problems overwhelming. But then we see a new potential or possibility and it is like the problems never existed. Often it is simply that we have heard God speak into our situation. Circumstances may not necessarily change, but when we know again that He is with us and sustaining us, our hope is restored.

Psalm 32 talks about a shift like that. There David writes about his own experience of forgiveness and its effects on His soul.

He is relating to his recent misadventures with Bathsheba, a woman he had secretly seduced and whose husband David had murdered. For months he had kept it quiet, and it was withering his soul.

> *When I kept silent, my bones wasted away*
> *through my groaning all day long. For day and*
> *night your hand was heavy on me; my strength*
> *was sapped as in the heat of summer.*[1]

Finally, God had shone a light on the situation through Nathan the prophet. He confronted David, pointing his finger at him saying, *"You are the man!"*[2]

Once God switches on these lights, a process has begun that must find its resolution. He highlights an area to be dealt with, gives us all we need to deal with it well, and sets us up for a future of freedom. That is His way – life and freedom.

David summarises his lessons in this way:

> *Do not be like the horse or the mule, which have*
> *no understanding but must be controlled by bit*
> *and bridle or they will not come to you. Many are*
> *the woes of the wicked, but the LORD's unfailing*
> *love surrounds the one who trusts in him*[3].

David had felt like a stubborn mule being dragged where he did not want to go. He didn't want to repent; the shame and punishment was more than he would volunteer for. But once the choice was taken from him, he embraced the process fully, relieved to be past the hiding.

When he had repented fully, he could joyfully say, *"the Lord's unfailing love surrounds the one who trusts Him"*[4].

David had experienced grace, and that grace had a rhythm. There were two beats in that rhythm; one from David, and one from God.

The first beat was repentance. God could not do that for David, it was his responsibility alone. The second beat was belief, or faith. He relied on God to both deal justly and give him strength to turn around. *"Unfailing love surrounds those who trust* (believe in) *Him"*, he said.

Repent and believe – that is the rhythm of grace for transformation. If you want to see change in your life, whether it be for a dealing with your brokenness or for aiming for a preferred future, this is the mechanism to follow.

When God shines a light on an area of our life to change, He is inviting us to repent and believe.

To repent means we need to turn, to literally invert the way we think and act. To believe means I rely on Him fully to give me grace – His empowering presence.

Jesus knew this rhythm of grace, too, and it was one of his frequent tools during His itinerant ministry. The gospel account says that He went throughout Galilee saying:

"The time has come; the kingdom of God has come near. Repent and believe the good news!"[5]

The process Jesus laid out there is a timeless recipe for transformation. This powerful rhythm of grace has brought freedom to the generations for millennia, and will continue to do so.

But notice the first few words in Jesus proclamation: *"The time has come"*.

For David, the time had come when Nathan pointed his convicting finger. For us, the time comes in a myriad of ways. God has a whole bank of lights He can shine on our lives, exposing that which is hidden that is slowly decaying our soul.

The word for time that Jesus used was the Greek word *kairos*, meaning an opportune moment, or proper season. He wasn't referring to the time of day, which is the word *chronos*. Jesus was saying, *"I am here, the season you have been waiting for is right now, grab it while you can"*.

What was up for grabs was the kingdom. It was there to be taken hold of for those who would repent and believe. The kingdom, of course, is the realm of God's dominion, the king's domain.

David reached out and grabbed the kingdom when his sin was exposed. He bowed before God, sought forgiveness and found life. The King of Heaven's dominion had just come to earth.

Jesus talks to you right now, just as He did back then. He is shining a light on an area of your life He wants to redeem. The time has come. Now is when you are to let Him fix it.

It is a *kairos* time, an opportunity to recognise and address a problem.

These *kairos* moments come at us all day. We may not have eyes to recognise them, but they are there. It is the moment your anger flares when you are cut off in traffic. It is the instant when your fear rises, threatening to choke you as your boss criticises your work. It may even be the bitter reaction you get when a friend lets you down badly.

They are like lights that get switched on, offering us an opportune moment to address a deeper issue. All fruit has a root – and it is the root that Jesus wants to address.

Let David's advice echo again. Before you switch those lights off rather than address what might be hidden, hear his hard-won wisdom:

> *Do not be like the horse or the mule, which have no understanding but must be controlled by bit and bridle or they will not come to you.*

It is time for you. What light has God been shining lately?

PRAYER

Lord, I know you have wanted to bring me to a more abundant life for a long time. What is it specifically that you are calling on me to address? Is there something blocking our relationship? What is slowly destroying my heart and relationships?

Help me see today with your eyes and heart.

Amen

REFERENCES

1. Psalm 32:3
2. Read the full account of David's confrontation and repentance in 2 Samuel 12
3. Psalm 32:9–10
4. Psalm 32:10
5. Mark 1:15

YOUR RESPONSE

Write down a short list of the things God has been trying to work out with you for some time. Then, ask God to shine a light on the one issue above all others that he wants to address in this season.

_____

_____

_____

3.2

One more night

Why did Pharaoh choose to sleep with the frogs one more night?

The account of his trouble in Exodus 8 makes no attempt at examining the man's inner world, other than to say his heart was hardened. But when God lets you determine the day of your deliverance, why would you choose tomorrow?

Why not now? Why not rid yourself of the pain and misery of having frogs in your bed, your bathroom, and even your coffee?

Let me take a guess – pride.

This imperceptive driver of the ambitious high-achievers will do almost anything to avoid being seen as out of control or defeated. By forestalling his deliverance, Pharaoh was saying, "*I don't need your help that much. I can take it. The problem isn't so bad that it has beaten me*".

When God turns up and shines a light on a problem, we retain the choice for how we respond. In fact, for most of us our default response it to carry on. The light itself seems to give us enough to cope with, let alone choosing to pause long enough to dig a little deeper.

When we are afraid, our energy is normally spent protecting ourselves. When we are ashamed, we do anything to cover up. When we are in pain, we will always gravitate to pleasure.

Pride will do anything to make itself look good, even if it is conducting a blatant hoax. Pharaoh could not have looked any more out of control, despite his bravado.

And so the familiar pain of our frogs is often chosen over the unfamiliar experience of encountering God and His dealings.

Sadly, avoidance only escalates issues, it never solves them. We always atrophy into deeper dysfunction. To grow requires intention and input – we don't drift into emotional health.

We all have our version of the frogs. They are our familiar issues – our beloved enemies. They are the broken parts of our nature that everyone else can see quite plainly but we think are either invisible or unimportant.

However, they are important to God if they are leading us to spiritual death or distance from Him. He knows better than we do what needs to be addressed.

And notably, the size of the issue is not related to the brightness of the light that shines on it. And we might also assume that the bigger the issue, the greater its obviousness. Not so.

Many of our negative mental constructs, inner wounds and emotional deficits have been in our life since childhood. Our earliest coping strategies can be invested in avoiding pain through separation, performance or manipulation. These become so familiar that they are completely normal to us, and to lose these mechanisms would infer loss of part of ourselves.

Whether or not we invest in error as a sin of ignorance, the ramifications are no less significant. And remember, God wants to deal with it because it is killing you, not because it is killing Him.

Sometimes grace is best manifested in raising an issue rather than looking beyond it.

Our avoidance, lack of urgency or genuine blindness can get in the way of a healing that God sees as vital for the fulfilment of our calling and health. And so God will continue to declare to us that *"The time has come, the kingdom is at hand, repent and believe"*[1].

However, continued avoidance on our part, particularly if it is not in ignorance, will be seen by God as a choice to invest in that activity. Slipping in to sin is one thing, but investment is seen as quite another. What we allow, we endorse.

> *Do not be deceived: God cannot be mocked. A man reaps what he sows. Whoever sows to please their flesh, from the flesh will reap destruction; whoever sows to please the Spirit, from the Spirit will reap eternal life.*[2]

We reap what we sow. This dynamic can in itself bring its own judgment, as our dysfunction degrades our soul to the point of suffering in our own private prison. In Romans 1, Paul describes this descent, saying multiple times that God *"gives us over"* to our own choices. And those choices lead to a greater experience of death.

We retain the right to choose. It is part of God's created order; He will not choose for you. And yet He will be as clear as possible on what we should choose.

What then is your prayer? *"God, make the light on my sin brighter"*, or *"God, put out that light"*.

The scriptures are loaded with *kairos* moments where God shone a light on people in the interest of turning them around.

King Nebuchadnezzar rejected his dream and Daniel's interpretation – but after seven years of calamity he came to his senses in repentance and belief.

The Apostle Paul was arrested by the brightest of lights as God knocked him off his high horse. He chose well and entered into the process of deep and lifelong change.

Pharaoh chose badly. Pride drove him to not only spend the night with the frogs but lose his army and credibility. He, and many more like him, defiantly reject God's offer all their life.

What is your response?

Jesus is saying now what He has always said: *"The kairos time has come!"* It is your time to change. It is your time to stop going around the same mountain, as familiar and safe as it might be.

It is time for you to break through.

PRAYER

Lord, I do not want to be investing in something that opposes your best for me. You know best, and you love me enough to want that which brings me life.

Today I pray you would open my eyes to anything that I have been prepared to tolerate, that you would not.

Amen

REFERENCES

1. Mark 1:15
2. Galatians 6:7–8

YOUR RESPONSE

What are the frogs that you have avoided dealing with? Think of the idols and slave drivers highlighted so far: what has been attached to that for too long, and needs to be cut off?

_____

_____

_____

_____

_____

_____

_____

_____

_____

_____

_____

3.3

Spotting a problem

Obviousness is in the eye of the beholder.

What seems clear to one person is hidden from another. The quirkiness or even fault we find in others seems plain, and yet from their own eyes it can be less apparent. Perhaps we get so comfortable with our ways that we no longer question or notice them.

Yet, when we see someone's dysfunction or questionable behaviour go on, we may hear ourselves say, *"How can God let them get away with that?"*

Sadly, we tend to judge others by their actions but ourselves by our intentions.

We know that for many of our failures there is an opposing and frustrated desire to do the right thing. That may or may not take the edge off our self-judgment, but we take a little solace by saying, *"That's a shame, but I meant well"*.

We don't see that inner battle in others, just the failures.

But what if we assessed ourselves through the external and clinical eyes of an observer? What if we did simply look at the fruit of our lives before we considered the inner struggles that preceded them?

Paul describes in Galatians 5:20 just a few of those observable fruit. He lists sexual immorality, impurity and debauchery; idolatry and witchcraft; hatred, discord, jealousy, fits of rage, selfish ambition, dissensions, factions and envy; drunkenness, and orgies.

If skimmed over quickly, we could dismiss any individual fault that we identify with, merely because it is in the presence of so many that seem deplorable. Surely the jealousy we feel can't be compared with debauchery? Paul must be talking about a more profound envy than the fleeting feelings I notice in myself?

No, he is not. Paul is talking about you and me.

Those "small issues" and fleeting feelings we allow in ourselves are listed next to some of the biggies of the sin index. Witchcraft is in the same sentence as ambition. Orgies are mentioned in the same breath as envy.

A reality check hits us, however, when we realise that those seemingly insignificant issues that we tolerate within our acceptable bandwidth of behaviour often become embedded. What we might label as big sins only happen occasionally and are inevitably followed by a proportional season of repentance. But the little issues are allowed to go under the radar.

Remember though that Paul puts them on the same list and at the same level. Then he goes further in the next chapter saying:

> *Do not be deceived: God cannot be mocked. A man reaps what he sows. Whoever sows to please their flesh, from the flesh will reap destruction.*[1]

If we cross the line from *slipping-into-sin* over to *sowing-into-sin*, then there are consequences. By sowing we mean that the behaviour and thinking are repeated and uncorrected. There is an investment or commitment to allow the condition to remain and grow.

What we allow, we condone. What we condone will grow.

I have noticed that God more often shines a light on the smaller, repeat offences in our life. The larger and more occasional issues are more often identified and dealt with quickly, through our own initiative.

Because it is God's light on the issue, and not our own, that light can be harder to distinguish. Like a warning signal on our car's dashboard, the indicator may be quite small. We should not correlate a smallness of the light to a smallness of the issue. God is simply being gracious and progressive in His dealings.

At first He will say, *"This is an issue, it is hurting you. You should allow me to deal with that"*. If we continue, He may even ask us, *"Will you deal with that?"*

Eventually, however, God will stop asking, and start telling you, *"Deal with that"*. Even then, He may be speaking in what we would regard His inside voice. In regard to sin, His outside voice is not one you want to hear, because that voice often declares His verdict on the issue.

In Daniel 4 there is an account of such dealings given first-hand by King Nebuchadnezzar. He had an issue with self-reliance and pride, and God had tried using an inside voice to get his attention. The King had a dream foretelling God's personal judgment and Daniel the prophet had interpreted it, warning the king that self-correction was needed.

Being proud, however, the king went on in self-admiration. A year later as he was declaring his own prowess, God let Nebuchadnezzar hear His outside voice. It was not a warning; it was a declaration of what was now going to happen. God would not be mocked!

And yet, even then, God's dealings were aimed at bringing the king to repentance and life. He experienced a severe mercy, being robbed of power and sanity for seven years until he could humble himself before God.

God is more committed to bringing us to fullness of life than we are. When He shines a light on our sin during our subtle *kairos* moments, His agenda is salvation for our inner world.

The bad fruit in our lives are not necessarily the problem, but they always point to the problem. Fruit always has a root. Trying to deal with fruit alone – cutting it off by will-power or discipline – will normally result in it growing back when our defences are down.

Jesus said it this way:

"No good tree bears bad fruit, nor does a bad tree bear good fruit. Each tree is recognised by its own fruit. People do not pick figs from thorn-bushes, or grapes from briers.

A good man brings good things out of the good stored up in his heart, and an evil man brings evil things out of the evil stored up in his heart. For the mouth speaks what the heart is full of.[2]

Before we go picking a fight with the slave drivers and idols in our life, it is wise to take stock and identify the actual fruit they produce in us.

As Jesus said, *"The time has come, the kingdom is at hand, repent and believe"*[3]. Will you grab this time – this season of opportunity – and look afresh at the fruit in your life that points to a deeper root?

PRAYER

I long, Lord, for the fruit of the Spirit to be evident in my life. I don't want to spend my life trying to merely trim off the bad; I long for the good!

Grant me the fruit of your Spirit today – the love, joy, peace and patience that comes from finding myself in you.

Amen

REFERENCES

1. Galatians 6:7–8
2. Luke 6:43–45
3. Mark 1:15

YOUR RESPONSE

You have already spent time considering your preferred future, and the things you believe God has been working on in your life. Perhaps there are other fruit in your life that do not seem to be connected to those things already listed. Take the time now to write down the recurring issues that, big or small, do not go away.

Approaching the no-go zone

READ FIRST: MARK 10:17–32

I wonder if you have ever gone away sad from Jesus' presence.

The idea seems unthinkable, and yet scripture has many accounts of those who turned their backs on Jesus.

Pontius Pilate asked Jesus to define truth but turned away before the answer came. Pharisees who saw miracles and heard irrefutable teaching remained stiff-necked and unwilling to bend.

Even though Jesus loved him, the rich ruler in today's scripture reading went away with his head low. He was unable to come to terms with the truth of where the treasure of his heart lay.

The man's face fell; it was too much to ask. His whole lifestyle and status was built on his wealth. To lose that would be to lose who he was. At least, that is how it felt.

He had come to Jesus prepared to deal with whatever was humanly possible. He had literally fallen on his knees, pleading for surety of a pure conscious. But Jesus had probed into a place that the young man presumed was beyond reasonable reach.

Jesus hit on a no-go zone. This is an area where we are not only blind to our faults, but there are so many protectors about us that any hint of threat is repelled my every mechanism possible.

The people around Jesus and the young ruler heard the exchange, and their reactions varied from amazement to fear[1]. They wondered if Jesus was withholding salvation from anyone whose surrender wasn't total. And yet we know that isn't the case. If it were, no-one could be saved. Salvation relies on what Jesus has done, not on what we have done.

But if we sign up to the transformation journey – and if we want the true freedom offered – then we need to realise that it is our no-go zones that will present the greatest challenge.

No-go zones are our perceived area of greatest personal threat. We guard them methodically and relentlessly. Many if not most people will go through their whole life dealing with a myriad of challenges and yet keep their no-go zones secure.

A no-go zone might be a particular man's determination to be someone or do something special. His inner world screams for validation, unmet as it should by people and God. His inner world is alone, bereft of consoling, side-tracked by the thrill of a victory, or even the hope of one.

In the absence of God in that place, he looks for an idol. He finds one called Power, and looks to it to fend off his pursuing slave driver called Humiliation. The people around him feel like pawns in his game, just an asset to bring about his plan. They feel used.

He struggles with anger, which is the fruit he can't explain. Every other part of his life is on-track. He might have an adoring family, financial security and a dedication to support his church. But he knows that, in regard to his status and drive, he just can't let Jesus in to threaten where his idol sits.

It is a part of him that is created by God to bring life, but that has become corrupted by brokenness. And it has become a no-go zone.

Or, it might be a particular woman who is blind to the insecurity-driven manipulations that she employs. In a thousand ways she adjusts conversations back to her. She is hoping for an instant relief from her self-doubts, so she fishes for affirmation or encouragement in any form. She will force people to befriend and comfort her.

Emotion and love had been withheld when she was a young child. In her heart she feels orphaned and weak, unable to pause long enough to find healing and grace through the offered Spirit of adoption. So she puts an idol of Approval in the place of God. She hears the constant threats of her slave driver called Rejection whom she must avoid at any cost.

When Jesus comes knocking on the door of her heart, He is welcomed in, but only so far. She will happily tell everyone about the grace she has received, but it remains a peripheral comfort. Her insecurity remains locked away. The thought of going there is too painful; it is her no-go zone.

If we want the truth, sometimes it is more productive to ask someone else to identify where our no-go zones are. Most of us have long since covered them up with instinctive safety mechanisms we can't even identify. Be assured, however, others can see them well enough.

The problem is that any friend willing to let you know may not be your friend for long! Most people will push such threats away. So let me help you identify them and, as you think and pray in to it, ask Jesus to show you what they may be.

No-go zones are often accompanied by our protectors – these are mechanisms of avoidance and safety. We develop whole coping strategies, even sections of personality to draw from or activate which keep us safe, and other people out.

We might have protectors as subtle as politeness or secrecy; passive-aggressive tools for avoiding any deep conversation. We might become deft at side-tracking conversations, or drawing attention to the faults of others.

Many people protect themselves through blame. Their walls come up and they look for a scapegoat, excuse or some obscure fault in others to focus on as the reason for their actions. What they feel is a sense of powerlessness to change, and so they place the responsibility for their dysfunction and healing on the shoulders of another.

Another common protector-set are those related to fear – fight, flight and freeze. When their no-go zone is challenged, they might come out swinging, or just run away emotionally. Whatever the response, they are avoiding dealing with their no-go zone.

People have a no-go zone because they are in an emotional and spiritual prison. They feel locked up, either by their own actions or those of another. In that sense they are prisoners or captives.

Jesus wants to set you free. He declared His mission clearly, citing Isaiah 61 when He said:

The Spirit of the Sovereign LORD is on me, because the LORD has anointed me to proclaim good news to the poor. He has sent me to bind up the broken-hearted, to proclaim

*freedom for the captives and release from darkness for
the prisoners, to proclaim the year of the LORD's favor.[2]*

Will you let Jesus do His job by shining a light into those
hidden places in your heart? The no-go zones are keeping
you bound, and your calling is to be free.

PRAYER

Lord, what rooms in my life have I kept you out of?

*I trust you enough to open the doors to the inner places, those
dark spaces where I suffer the most pain and shame. Where there
is fear, bring faith. Where there is shame, bring your acceptance.
Where there is judgment, grant me the grace to forgive.*

*Shine a light on the darkest places today Lord, and lead me to
freedom.*

REFERENCES

1. Mark 10:32
2. Isaiah 61:1–2

YOUR RESPONSE

What are your no-go zones? Why do you think they have been kept off limits for so long?

_____

_____

_____

_____

_____

_____

_____

_____

_____

_____

_____

_____

_____

3.5

What is the alternative?

READ FIRST: JOHN 21

"I have failed. It is over for me."

Simon Peter knew these feelings. They had tagged him all his life. His mouth regularly made promises his character couldn't fulfil.

Different setting, same Simon.

He had over-promised and under-delivered. Simon had vowed to Jesus in the Garden of Gethsemane that even if all others deserted Him, he never would[1]. All the disciples had heard it, and they knew all too well what happened next. Desertion, rejection, disownment – all before the rooster crowed.

Now they were gathered around the fire. Fish was on the menu, but there was an elephant in the room.

Jesus had risen and he met the disciples as they came in from fishing[2]. The symbolism was lost on no-one. They had caught nothing, but Jesus told them to cast out the nets one more time.

Jesus had done this before, three years earlier. That first time Simon had responded with fear – seeing the immanence of God and being aware of his sin. "Depart from me Lord, I am a sinful man"[3].

This time, rather than ask Jesus to keep His distance, Simon jumped out of the boat to get to Him. Jesus was calling Simon, reminding him through this repeated act that His plans for him had not changed. Despite his failure, Jesus still called Simon to become more like Peter. The wispy reed needed to become more of a rock[4].

Between those two similar events, Jesus had tried to give Simon numerous course corrections, but he wouldn't listen. *"Get behind me Satan"*, Jesus had said when Simon pushed an agenda that was contrary to God's plan[5].

Sometimes, if you won't stop, the world itself will stop you.

It is a shocking moment when that happens. You feel bereft of possibilities because the plans you had were all based in doing thing the way you always have. Simon's way was to promise big and push hard. But for all his pushing, he had achieved nothing.

What was the alternative?

It is a shame when we only ask this question as a last resort. Simon had hit a wall, but only because he had refused to stop running in the same direction for years. There was another way and now he was forced to look at it, if only because he had no other option.

He knew that even though his intentions and plans were rooted in good ideals, they could not succeed with his own strength. He just couldn't do it, and neither can you. Jesus was clear on this, saying:

> *"Remain in me, as I also remain in you. No branch can bear fruit by itself; it must remain in the vine. Neither can you bear fruit unless you remain in me. I am the vine; you are the branches. If you remain in me and I in you, you will bear much fruit; apart from me you can do nothing".[6]*

So, for Simon and Jesus it was time to clear the air. *"Do you love me more than the others here Simon?"* Three times Jesus probed. Simon had promised that he did love Jesus more, but he had demonstrated otherwise.

Now the cavalier bravado was gone. Simon knew his limitations. He had once promised unconditional love, now the word he used for love was that of brotherly affection.

It was sincere love, yet limited. This was all Simon had. He knew that now, but he gave it to Jesus.

"Then feed my lambs", Jesus said. Simon's calling to lead was intact, but it was not to be based in his own abilities. It was to be centred in, and sourced from, his connection with Jesus. It was a ministry from the inside out, the Spirit doing what Simon could never do on his own.

In Acts 2 we see what this looked like for Simon. The Spirit came there in power, giving Simon a voice that was way beyond his own. He preached and thousands were saved. This became the pattern for his life – God's power, God's fruit.

That was the alternative for Simon. What is yours?

You have looked hard in the previous chapters at the various elements of your life that might need to be addressed. Like Simon, you have had your *kairos* moments, but can you see the alternative?

At every opportune time to change, God's alternative is available.

"The time has come; the kingdom is at hand," Jesus said. *"Reach out and grab it!"*[7].

The kingdom, and all it brings for us, is predominantly a state of heart. The kingdom is where God's will be done – it is where He is king. Jesus said that the kingdom is not something to be observed, because it is within you[8].

The long list of bad fruit listed in Galatians 5 are behaviours that are observable. But Paul goes on to list the alternative fruits of God's Spirit, and they are all internal. God doesn't focus on behaviour; He focuses on your heart. He knows that if your heart changes, your life changes.

He lists some of those fruits – gentleness, goodness, meekness, love and so on. All inward attributes. In Romans 14:17 Paul gets even more precise saying, *"The kingdom of God is not eating and drinking (outward acts), but of righteousness, peace and joy in the Holy Spirit"*.

Did you notice that? The kingdom of God is found *in* the Holy Spirit.

That is your alternative – a change of heart by the power of God's Spirit.

How might that look for you? How could this all turn out if God had His way in you fully?

Failure is not an obligation for you anymore. You can change. You should change. But if you were to change, what would it look like?

What is the alternative?

PRAYER

Father, even when I fail, you pursue me. In my darkest and weakest moments, you come to me. You wash me clean and set me back on the path of righteousness.

Lord I thank you that you are love, and all you do in me is because you love me. Thank you, Lord, that you never let me go.

Amen

REFERENCES

1. Matthew 26:33–35
2. John 21
3. Luke 5:4–10
4. Simon means reed. Peter (Greek: petros, meaning Rock)
5. Matthew 16:23
6. John 15:4–5
7. Mark 1:15
8. Luke 17:21

YOUR RESPONSE

What is on offer for you to replace the issues God is wanting
to address? What fruit of the Spirit could overrule the fruit
of the old nature? If you could ask God for one thing in this
regard, what would it be?

_____

_____

_____

_____

_____

_____

_____

_____

_____

_____

_____

_____

_____

Placing everything on the table

READ FIRST: LUKE 19:1–9

When people experience salvation, something inevitably changes on the inside.

Some people remember the moment they placed their faith in Christ and He entered their bereft world to bring light and love for the first time.

But salvation is an ongoing affair. We go on being saved until the day when we inherit the fullness of that salvation. As we navigate this in-between time, we experience moments of salvation where Jesus sets us free from the bonds of sin and brokenness.

The original Greek word for saved that is used so often through the New Testament is *sozo*. It means to save, heal and deliver. It has thorough implications, relating to the potential for freedom for our "whole-person".

For the whole-person to be saved, the whole-person needs to be on the table.

To have everything on the table is a phrase used to imply that everything is open for negotiation, nothing is hidden, and all is up for consideration. If we want Jesus to bring us to the life he so clearly promised, then He needs access to all of us.

When Jesus was passing through the ancient city of Jericho, he knew the history. It was known as the place where Joshua and God's people had to walk around until God tore down the walls.

Jesus was about to tear down a few walls of his own; all he needed to find was a heart with a glimmer of willingness to be saved.

With a hunter's gleam, Jesus spotted little Zacchaeus in the tree and took His shot. He didn't wait for Zacchaeus to be totally holy before building a bridge into his life. *"Hey Zacchaeus, you get to feed me and my friends tonight!"*

Jesus treated Zacchaeus as one who already belonged. As the evening progressed, he came to believe in Jesus, placing his faith in Him. Only then did Zacchaeus' behaviour take a shift. He belonged first, then believed, then ultimately behaved.

Unlike the rich young ruler who turned away sad when Jesus mentioned His wealth, Zacchaeus took the first step. He laid it all on the table – his money, his reputation and his life. And he did it with a smile. He was a man with nothing to lose.

> *"Look, Lord! Here and now I give half of my possessions to the poor, and if I have cheated anybody out of anything, I will pay back four times the amount." Jesus said to him, "Today salvation has come to this house …"*[1]

No one quite dances or smiles like the person who is free. No one is totally free when they still have things they are not prepared to lose. It still owns them, and therefore they are a slave to it.

A person who wants to be free has nothing left to hide or protect. The prize on offer is so valuable to them that any life, or any death for that matter, is worth trading in for it.

Imagine what went through the Apostle Paul's mind when he was first confronted with the truth that Jesus was Lord. It went against absolutely everything he believed, fought for and relied upon for his standing before God. His total worldview imploded as he realised that everything he had pursued relentlessly for his whole life was actually futile.

When Jesus knocked Paul off his high horse, he had to be prepared to put all or nothing on the table. Give access to it all, or walk away.

You may well have come to that place as you have worked through this book.

Only those who are willing are able to experience the life on offer. That willingness plays out on a few levels.

Firstly, we must be willing to stop and listen to God.

This is a rare attribute, even among God's people. The momentum of life, the structure of our culture, and our determination to stay in a direction we previously found acceptable all conspire to keep our ears shut.

Secondly, we must be willing to turn. As Paul himself made clear:

> *"Whenever anyone turns to the Lord, the veil is taken away. Now the Lord is the Spirit, and where the Spirit of the Lord is, there is freedom."*[2]

We must be prepared to turn away from our own strength and our own way of doing things.

That turning will require us to change the way we think and act. Our old ways of living will always result in the same outcome. Often there are kingdom keys to be found here that remain hidden from those who are not prepared to bend or obey.

Proverbs 25:2 says that *"It is the glory of God to conceal a matter; to search out a matter is the glory of kings"*. God doesn't hide things from us, but for us. It is the journey to finding them that helps us grow. We search these keys out by taking a turn from our old path and seeking the will and way of God for a new way forward.

One of these transformative keys of the kingdom is forgiveness. This principle alone can unlock lives that previously have been held captives to the abuse, neglect or misrepresentation of others. By clearing the person's debt to us, we release them into God's hands for Him to deal with as Judge.

As we seek God on an issue that holds us back, ask Him frequently about who it is you have to forgive! The answer may surprise you and set you free!

Finally, once our willingness to turn has led us to a point of recognition of the true problem, we must be willing to surrender. We come to a point where our old ways of thinking and behaving need to bow to the cross of Christ. Zacchaeus did that and found true life for the first time.

How about you? Is it all on the table with nothing to hide?

This is your time. The kingdom is at hand. Take it, whatever the cost, and find salvation in a whole new way.

Prayer

Lord, is there someone I need to forgive? Is there an issue I have been unwilling to put on the table?

Will you show me why I have done that? Show me the problem Lord, and lead me to more abundant life.

Amen

References

1. Luke 19:8–9
2. 2 Corinthians 3:16–17

Your response

Is there anything you have struggled to put on the table? List it here for your own confession, and ask yourself why it has been so important to you.

_____

_____

_____

_____

_____

_____

Can you honestly say that everything in your life is now on the table?

_____

_____

_____

_____

_____

_____

_____

_____

_____

_____

_____

_____

_____

Group Session 4

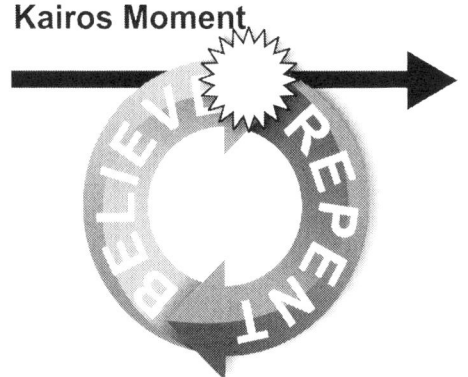

Kairos moments are an invitation to come off the path of life that has gotten you to this point, and to grow through a new level of engagement with God.

This week you will have been confronted with a choice: to change or not to change.

Your decision will be determined by your desire. What do you want to do? Will you stay the same or will you grow? God leaves that choice in your hands.

Q. How would you describe your desire given what you know now?

Retreat and advance

For participants who attended a spiritual retreat in the last week.

The days following a time of spiritual refreshment can be somewhat difficult to navigate. Disengaging from normality to spend time with God and His people gives a unique and somewhat unsustainable opportunity to extend our hearts in a deliberate mountain-top experience.

Every mountain casts its own shadow. What happens on Monday when we re-engage with the life we left behind? The same people, problems and stresses are waiting for us. Were my gains valid? What if I didn't experience what I was hoping for? All sorts of questions come to mind.

Good! That is what is supposed to happen. Mountain tops give us a new vision for what normal can look like if we grow over time.

It is not practical to breathe the rarified air of the summit indefinitely – and so we must allow ourselves to fall back and recover. To grow in any area, we must extend past our present sustainable limit, then enter a phase of re-creation. There our spirit grows and adapts, ready to extend again.

This is what a "rhythm of grace" is all about!

Q. What questions and thought processes have arisen in response to your spiritual retreat?

_____

YOUR RESPONSES FROM THE PAST WEEK

What, in this opportune moment God has given you, have you identified to change? Share with each other your responses to chapters 3.1 thru 3.4

> **3.1** Write down a short list of the things God has been trying to work out with you for some time. Then, ask God to shine a light on the one issue above all others that He wants to address in this season.

> **3.2** What are the frogs that you have avoided dealing with? Think of the idols and slave drivers highlighted so far – what has been attached to that for too long, and needs to be cut off?

> **3.3** You have already spent time considering your preferred future, and the things you believe God has been working on in your life. Perhaps there are other fruit in your life that do not seem to be connected to those things already listed. Take the time now to write down the recurring issues that, big or small, do not go away.

3.4 What are your no-go zones? Why do you think they have been kept off limits for so long?

Repentance requires us to turn from one way of thinking towards something new. What is the alternative future that is on offer to you? Share your response from chapter 3.5.

3.5 What is on offer for you to replace the issues God is wanting to address? What fruit of the Spirit could overrule the fruit of the old nature? If you could ask God for one thing in this regard, what would it be?

Is everything on the table for you? Are you prepared to give God access to every part of your life? If you are not, why is that? If you are, what have you had to give God access to that previously has been off-limits? Share your responses to chapter 3.6

3.6 Is there anything you have struggled to put on the table? List it here for your own confession, and ask yourself why it has been so important to you.

Can you honestly say that everything in your life is now on the table?

PRAY FOR EACH OTHER

Spend some time praying for each member of the group. Ask God to give them clarity and grace for their next steps in the journey to transformation and spiritual empowerment.

4.1

A rhythm of grace

READ FIRST: MATTHEW 11:25–30

Are you tired yet?

You have probably been a Christian for some time now. You know the rules. You have an idea how you are supposed to behave.

You have given it your best shot. You have been faithful and tried your hardest to get it right. You know you are forgiven, and you thank God for that because your efforts at getting better just keep coming up short.

Some days you don't even get close.

You seem to be scared of the same things as everyone else. You struggle with the same temptations. You judge those around you. If people could look in to your private world, you would probably be horrified.

Take heart – the good news is the same as the bad news! You can't fix yourself!

That is why Jesus offers grace. Listen to His words:

Are you tired? Worn out? Burned out on religion? Come to me. Get away with me and you'll recover your life. I'll show you how to take a real rest. Walk with me and work with me—watch how I do it.

Learn the unforced rhythms of grace. I won't lay anything heavy or ill-fitting on you. Keep company with me and you'll learn to live freely and lightly.[1]

Jesus wasn't giving us permission to never deal with our bad stuff. Living freely and lightly could not look like that. Of course, there will always be parts of your life you want to see transformed – but perfection isn't the theme here.

What Jesus is saying is that you can rest from the burden of trying to perform from your own strength, or living up to a perceived standard. If you do, you will just be constantly tired and worn out. You will be disillusioned and discouraged.

Jesus' solution is grace – the rhythms of grace, to be exact.

Grace is not just forgiveness, or justification. They are certainly acts of grace, but the word itself is much bigger than that. The Greek for grace, *charis*, can be best defined as *empowering presence.*

Prior to Christians getting hold of the word, *charis* was used to explain the idea of an external influence which brought about a change, often to a person. God's grace gives us forgiveness of sin, redemption and access to our heavenly Father. That changes everything!

The gifts of the Spirit mentioned in the New Testament are called *charisma* in the Greek text, meaning gifts of grace. Paul also calls them spiritual gifts, using the word we now know so well, *pneumatikos*[2]. Where the Spirit of God is, there is grace, God's empowering presence.

The point here is that you are not alone.

You have never been able to do much of worth under your own steam, and that will never change. But Christ in you can do anything because He has no such limits[3]. What is more, God gives us His Spirit without limit![4]

And if the Spirit of him who raised Jesus from the dead is living in you, he who raised Christ from the dead will also give life to your mortal bodies because of his Spirit who lives in you. Therefore, brothers and sisters, we have an obligation—but it is not to the flesh, to live according to it.[5]

You probably already know this, right?

What then is the problem? If all this power is on offer, why can we not tap in to it?

The issue cannot be on God's side of the equation since He has declared that the limits are off. The problem is not that He is withholding, but that we are not quite able to hold on to Him.

He wants us to work with Him, and walk with Him. That means that in the process of our transformation God is not independent and nor are we. It is a partnership, a form of co-labouring. Some have even called it a dance where Jesus leads and we keep in step.

I like to use the term rhythms of grace, as used in the Message version of Matthew 11:28–29. *"Walk with me and work with me, watch how I do it. Learn the unforced rhythms of grace."*

Rhythms have a cadence to them, an easy and predictable pace. These rhythms allow us to work in close unison with God to do and be what He calls us to. Like a dance, they require us to be involved – we do our part, and God does His. Each partner is dependent on the other to what only they should do.

In these rhythms we push forward and then we pull back. We do what we should with the little strength we have but then we rest in God, relying on His strength to bear the fruit required.

Remember, we are dust and we are breath. To live as we are called, we must learn how these two elements work together.

To overcome the habits, thinking and wounds of our old nature, there is a specific rhythm of grace to apply. We looked at it in previous chapters without labelling it as such. It is found in Mark 1:15:

> *"The time has come", he said. "The kingdom of God has come near. Repent and believe the good news!"*

You may have missed it. The key words are repent and believe. That is the rhythm. Our side of the equation is to repent – that is where our work comes in. But then we believe – we rely on God, we rest in His strength to do what only He can do.

Most of us see repentance as just turning away from something. But there is more – we actually turn to something as well. We put off one thing and put on another.

We also turn to God. In him is the strength found to live the abundant life Jesus offered.

Are you tired of doing it alone? Have you struggled to find God's strength when you need it? Then this is the journey for you – a rhythm of grace where the kingdom can come to every area of your life.

PRAYER

Lord, it is time for me. I have tried to do things alone because I haven't known how to draw from your grace.

Thank you for never letting go. Show me how to work with you and walk with you in a whole new way. I need your grace; show me your ways that I may walk in them.

Amen.

REFERENCES

1. Matthew 11:28–29 MSG
2. 1 Corinthians 12:1; 4
3. Colossians 1:27
4. John 3:34
5. Romans 8:11–12

YOUR RESPONSE

Where have you experienced spiritual tiredness? What have been the struggles you are unable to overcome in your own strength?

_____

_____

4.2

Repentance

The reason that people do things that contradict their new nature in Christ is because they are not thinking with the mind of Christ.

The human mind is the gateway to the spiritual realm. If you believe the lies of Satan, you are in effect choosing to be in partnership with that spirit. Therefore, it is his spiritual influence that you will feel at your back, blowing you towards that which fills your thoughts.

But 1 Corinthians 2:16 says that we have the mind of Christ. Paul later puts it another way saying, *"We take captive every thought to make it obedient to Christ"*[1].

In context, that scripture is talking about the Christian's biggest weapon in spiritual warfare – a transformed mind.

In Romans 12:2, Paul says we are transformed by renewing our mind – by changing the way we think.

Just as we can choose to align our thinking with our enemy, we can of course align it with our Friend and Strengthener, Jesus Christ. By agreeing with the way He thinks, we open ourselves to receiving His wind at our backs.

One of the key disciplines attached to repentance is that of confession.

To confess is not merely the act of owning up to wrongdoing. Confession is deeper, bringing with it a sense of agreement. To confess to Christ is to agree with Him that my corrupted thinking is counter to His path to life. A confession can also be defined as a way of thinking or even a set of doctrinal beliefs.

To repent means to turn around and head the other way. We turn our actions and, even more importantly, our thinking to resemble that of Christ. We choose to see things His way.

Repentance calls on us to see our world from Christ's perspective. "Re" means to go back and "Pent" refers to the topmost place – the *pent*house! We are to get our thinking back to the perspective of heaven.

Since, then, you have been raised with Christ,
set your hearts on things above, where Christ is,

seated at the right hand of God. Set your minds
on things above, not on earthly things.²

Note there how Paul seamlessly connects the human heart with the human mind. The two are in constant organic union, with the cries of the heart inciting the mind to find strategies to have its needs met.

When the heart is sick, the mind finds ways to try and find peace. If we think from the wrong perspective, however, seeking to have our needs met in carnal ways, then we disengage from the power of God's Spirit.

In your scripture reading today you will have noted that:

What we have received is not the spirit of the
world, but the Spirit who is from God, so that we
may understand what God has freely given us.³

God's Spirit within not only gives us the power to live well, He gives us access to the perspective of heaven on who we are. In that way we can understand or, in other words, think clearly on who we are.

Repentance is not merely turning away from something; it is turning to something else.

Our *kairos* moments are the opportunity to turn off the path of life we are currently on. We have the opportune moment to look at things differently, to ask of God, *"What is the problem here, Lord?"* or *"What do you think about this?"*

This is the beginning of the rhythm of grace we call Repent and Believe.

I once heard a young man explain this so well from his own life. He had previously suffered under a pervasive addiction to pornography and sexual sin. After God had done a truly transformative work within him, restoring his heart, his family and his dignity, he found himself tempted once again.

His eyes glanced over at the figure of an attractive woman and the old feelings of desire began to threaten him quickly. But he thought, *"Hang on, this isn't me. I have dealt with the reasons for my past failure. What is the problem here Lord?"*

He immediately recognised in himself a tension that resides in most men, that of pursuit to a conquest. He had endured a long, hard week of counselling and was drained. He hadn't had a tangible win for a long time.

In the beauty he saw before him, he saw an opportunity to pursue, to flirt, to grasp what was out of reach. It wasn't about sex at all; he wanted to chase and win! By thinking clearly, he was able to see things from God's perspective. He wasn't broken, he was a normal man who needed to meet his needs in more godly ways.

His solution was to take his boat on the lake to catch a fish
– and it worked! He was close to God, blessed his wife with
fish for dinner, and had a personal win all at the same time.

True repentance always puts off an old way of thinking
and replaces it with the new.

Sometimes the answer is obvious, or easily heard. At other
times we need to seek longer, and go deeper.

Think then of the issues you are facing right now. What is
your *kairos* moment? Whatever it is, it presents you with the
option of transformation into abundant life.

You may not get all the answers quickly, but the answers
are there. Will you turn off the road you are on and into the
rhythm of grace where God works with you to change?

PRAYER

*Lord, what is the problem? How am I thinking wrongly about
myself or about you?*

*I have repeatedly fallen into the same patterns for some time
now, thinking wrongly about my life. I confess this to you now, and
want to come in to agreement with what you say about me.*

Lord, what might be the problem?

Amen.

REFERENCES

1. 2 Corinthians 10:5
2. Colossians 3:1–2
3. 1 Corinthians 2:12

YOUR RESPONSE

In regard to the issue you have chosen to address, what might be the wrong thinking that has led to that being a longstanding part of your life?

What lies might you believe about yourself, or about God? Where do you need to turn your thinking?

_____

_____

_____

_____

_____

_____

_____

_____

Looking behind the idol

READ FIRST: ROMANS 1:18–32

Why do we reason in foolish ways?

In the previous chapter you were asked to seek God about where you need to change your thinking. I wonder what He told you and if it surprised you.

I continually encourage people to ask God those sorts of questions. And God seems incredibly enthusiastic to answer in so many cases!

Identifying our wrong thinking is such an incredible start on the path to repentance. But if we want to undergo permanent transformation, we need to go deeper.

We need to look at why we think the way we do and address the root which brings forth such consistent fruit.

In the scripture reading for this chapter, Paul describes the slippery slope of those who end up displaying all the destructive fruit that you may recognise in the world today. The symptoms seldom change much, despite the passing of centuries.

You may even identify with a few of them: sexual deviation, greed, envy of others, deceit, slander, arrogance, even disobeying parents gets a mention.

What is helpful to recognise is the process we follow that results in such unpalatable fruit. It has not changed since the beginnings of human history, and it continues to happen before our eyes. If you can spot the fruit, it is easy to follow the root.

The problem always starts when humanity tries to meet valid needs in invalid ways. We are made to be blessed, living from the inheritance God ordained for us. Those blessings are sourced through God, but since the fall we have looked for alternate ways to realise what our spirit is designed to enjoy.

With or without intimate connection with God, the design He wove into our hearts remains. We have needs for identity, security and meaning. Satan offers counterfeit ways to meet those needs and his version always counters a relationship with God.

Everything within God's design is hinged on our relationship with Him. The moment we separate, or have our needs met in exclusion of Him, we become unhinged.

Satan does not even care if you bury yourself in work for God. If he can get you more consumed in that than your actual walk with God, then he has succeeded.

Romans 1:21–23 says that humanity disconnected from God; therefore, their thinking lost heavenly perspective. Their design remained however, and so they looked for ways to have their needs met. Eventually they turned to their idols – images made to replicate themselves or the "spirit" of their tribe.

The first result of that we see in Romans 1 was deep-seated sexual impurity. They lost intimacy with God and tried to meet their need through objectified and ever-more-risky sexual practices. Does that not sound like the world we live in that has "rationally" explained away the existence of God?

Romans 1 goes further. They not only lost relationship but verse 28 says they lost the actual knowledge of God. Now, not only did they not know God, they did not even know about Him.

Their mind was disconnected from truth, and so the implications of that began to multiply into all the fruit that we see to this day.

It all begun with disconnection from God – an orphaned spirit. From that place of perceived abandonment, human beings seek out an alternative to worship, and seek provision or safety without God.

Habitual sexual sin is often the fruit of a disconnected heart.

Pain always seeks pleasure, and if our hearts are alone, or in pain, we will attempt to replace the long-term fruits of the love received from a deep relationship with an attempt at immediate gratification through physical or mental stimulation.

To change, we need to become expert at looking behind the idols in our life.

You might remember that the first two commandments say that there shall be no other gods before the Lord, and no idols. You can now see why!

Only God can meet the needs of our heart that He Himself put there. An idol can only offer to forestall the ache in our hearts for deep intimacy and meaning from God Himself. Our hearts are made for Him.

Sexual sin is different to every other destructive behaviour. It is a physical action that has a doorway into our very spirits, and a potential stronghold for the evil one to take advantage of. It seeks to replace the presence of God in our hearts with an idol of temporary stimulation. In that way it can effectively destroy our soul piece by piece.

Scripture, based in the premise that sexual activity unites us fully to another person, body, soul and spirit, tells us:

Whoever is united with the Lord is one with him in spirit.

Flee from sexual immorality. All other sins a person commits are outside the body, but whoever sins sexually, sins against their own body. Do you not know that your bodies are temples of the Holy Spirit, who is in you, whom you have received from God?[1]

All sins can be forgiven. All spiritual damage can be healed by our gracious God. But do not think that simply confessing sin is enough to heal your broken heart.

We need to go deeper than the fruit, to discover and deal with the dark root.

We need to look behind the idols and discover what needs we are trying to meet through them and why. Only then can we experience the freedom of deep repentance and healing.

In the absence of deep intimacy with God, our human spirits operate as orphans – afraid, alone and in pain.

It is, however, merely a self-imposed veil that separates us from God in this way. He has already paid the price to join with us at an ever-deeper level. All we need do is turn to Him in full understanding and repentance.

> *Whenever anyone turns to the Lord, the veil is taken away. Now the Lord is the Spirit, and where the Spirit of the Lord is, there is freedom.*[2]

In chapter 1.4 you identified some potential idols in your life. What were they? Further than that, what lies or replacements for God's provision might lie behind them?

PRAYER

Lord, what is behind the idols I have turned to? I do not want them anymore; I want only you. Show me why I have bought in to the lies of these idols and the spirit behind them. Shine a light on every dark place that has become a stronghold of disconnection from you.

Amen.

REFERENCES

1. 1 Corinthians 6:17–19
2. 2 Corinthians 3:16–17

YOUR RESPONSE

In chapter 1.4 you identified an idol that you bow to. What is it? Why do you think it has come to have the place in your life that it does? Is there a lie you have believed and need to repent of?

_____

_____

_____

_____

_____

_____

_____

_____

_____

_____

_____

_____

_____

_____

4.4

Dishonour

READ FIRST: MATTHEW 10:40–42

Have you ever felt like those closest to you are the last to see your potential? Perhaps you can sense that people have put you in a box based on your failures. Or, maybe you are hemmed in by your workmates' perceptions of who you can be.

You are not alone. Jesus had the same problem.

Yes, even Jesus!

During the high point of his ministry life, Jesus passed through the area where He spent most of His life. The people there had seen Him grow from boyhood – watched him play with their own children. They saw Him learn a trade and make furniture. They knew all about Jesus, or so they assumed.

Based on their judgment of Jesus, they dishonoured Him. *"Why is Jesus acting like our teacher when we have been with Him since childhood?"*[1]

Dishonour is something God takes incredibly seriously.

He has designed the relational order of the kingdom in such a way that genuine honouring of God and people facilitates blessing in our lives. Jesus was in town to share the gospel and demonstrate the kingdom. Wherever He went, people were always healed and set free.

But not now, not here in His hometown. That kingdom power was literally extinguished by the response of those who devalued and doubted Him.

> *Jesus said to them, "A prophet is not without honor except in his own town, among his relatives and in his own home."*
>
> *He could not do any miracles there, except lay his hands on a few sick people and heal them. He was amazed at their lack of faith.*

Our lives are directly affected by the way we value other people. If the blessing that Jesus came to give can be shut down, so can anyone else's.

We are created to bless the world and to receive the blessing of others. The implications of this on us personally are deep and wide. Our choice to dishonour people robs us of the blessings we need to thrive, even as children.

This topic is raised in the context of this book because repentance of our choice to dishonour people can restore to our lives the blessings our hearts need to thrive.

Consider your scripture reading from Matthew 10:40–42. When Jesus refers to us welcoming someone, He is talking about honour. Some translations even use the word honour in place of welcome.

He says that if we honour those who come in Jesus' name, we honour Jesus Himself and receive the reward of that. If we honour one of Jesus' appointed leaders, then we receive the blessings God releases through such a person. Jesus says that even children, if honoured properly, bring with them a certain reward.

This principle has implications in how we deal with those in authority over us, and throughout many other areas of life.

But the deepest implications in the context of your spiritual health relate to how you have dealt with your family of origin.

Paul draws on the implications of the 5th commandment when He says:

Children, obey your parents in the Lord, for this is right.
"Honor your father and mother"—which is the first
commandment with a promise—"so that it may go well
with you and that you may enjoy long life on the earth."[3]

From our youngest years, children have a bias to not only do their own thing but to resent being controlled. Inwardly, too, children are forced to confront the imperfections of their parents and the implications that has on their childish heart.

Neglect, abuse, bad example and a myriad of other mistakes bombard the child's spirit. And, piece by piece, many of us build an inner storehouse of dishonour against our parents.

Mistakenly we see honour as something we cannot give because we too tightly associate honour with obedience – and yet the two are separate. You can be honouring to parents or leaders while choosing not to follow their directives if they go against the known will of God.

In its earliest form, to honour parents meant that a person lived a life of such quality that people would reflexively hold their parents in high regard. *"Wow, they must have had great parents to become like that!"*

Many of us struggle to honour our parents fully, often with good reason. And yet the blessings and inner thriving we are meant to inherit are so often activated by that very principle. We might wonder why life actually does not *"go well for us"*, as the commandment promises, and overlook the bind we are locked in that comes from our devaluing of those closest to us.

Early on we might have made a secret inner vow to never be like our parents. We might resolve to hold a grudge, or even punish them with our own rebellion. In a thousand ways we reject their example because of lack of honour. And, as such, it is us who continues to suffer.

God doesn't call us to honour bad behaviour or abuse. But He does expect us to honour people's position in relation to us. His created order is such that our relationship with God is foremost, but our relationship with others creates the dynamic for experiencing the fullness of blessing.

He was clear on our priorities in life: love God passionately, and love people as we would love ourselves[4]. That can be tough. In fact, it is impossible without God's help.

Often dishonour is what sits behind the idols of our life. Ambition, isolation, self-reliance and control are idols we bow to if we are disconnected from people and the blessings they bring.

We need to repent of the inner vows we have taken which lock us out from our inheritance in this life.

How do you regard those in authority over you, in particular your parents? Could there be an area where you need to reassess your way of thinking about them or yourself?

Prayer

Lord, please show me if there are ways I have dishonoured the people you have placed all around me. Have I valued them the way I am called to? Is there reward and blessing that is withheld through dishonour? If so, how might I show true fruit of my repentance?

Amen.

References

1. Mark 6:3
2. Mark 6:4–6
3. Ephesians 6:1–3
4. Mark 29:28–31

Your response

Perhaps the issue of dishonour is not one that you need to consider. If you have prayed and feel that you hold everyone in the level of regard that God expects, then enjoy the rewards of that. However, if God has raised an issue for you to deal with, write it down here and include your prayerful response in how to deal with it.

4.5

Offence

READ FIRST: MATTHEW 18:21–35

Jesus took the issues of honour and forgiveness seriously. Very seriously!

In fact, honour and forgiveness are intrinsically connected. In the passage from Mark 6 we looked at in the previous chapter, Jesus could not release blessings because of an absence of honour. That dishonour was manifested in a thing called offence.

> "… Isn't this the carpenter? …" And they **took offence** at him.
>
> Jesus said to them, "A prophet is not **without honour** except in his own town …" He could not do any miracles there … "[1]

189

Offence is what happens when you combine judgment with unforgiveness. We make up our mind that someone is in the wrong and we hold it against them. Jesus said that the offence held against Him was a facet of dishonour and therefore the people did not receive what could have been theirs.

Many of us live for decades without living in the full expression of blessing and favour that God offers us – especially in our hearts. And while we do not actually earn most of God's blessings, since they are freely offered, we can choose to reject or even cut ourselves off from them.

So much of what God can do in us is available, and yet not automatic.

He offers fullness of His Spirit, and yet so few Christians experience that. He offers salvation, but the majority of people reject it.

The peace, joy and purpose that come from a Spirit-empowered life are available to all, and yet there are issues that block us from realising that.

It may surprise you to know that our tendencies of dishonour and offence are two of the most common reasons for a dysfunctional or stagnant spiritual life.

If you begin a journey of discovering why you cannot move on from an issue, or are locked in a behaviour, the process of transformation may well result in you asking God, "*Who do I need to forgive?*"

Let me explain.

Say, for example, you are locked in a performance mentality that drives you to do well at something in order to feel good about yourself. You have come to that place because of years spent living in accordance with an inner vow – a secret promise you have said to yourself. You may have said, "*I will do better than the rest, because then I will know I am worth something*". Or, "*If I do really well at this, someone will notice*".

Why might you have constructed that inner vow? Probably because your needs for significance, identity or security were not being adequately met by the situation you were in. You mother may not have given enough comfort, or your father may have been absent or hard to please.

Whatever the reason, you have proceeded down a path of trying to rationally meet the needs of your wounded spirit by constructing a life that eases that pain. But the relief is at best temporary. In the absence of healing you will need to re-discover that stimulation over and over.

At the root is an inner vow that has made you stumble – an offence, rooted in dishonour that has blocked access to the love and intimacy of your Heavenly Father. To remedy the situation, you need to remove the blockage by forgiving the one who incited your judgment.

This is repentance – a change in the way you think that aligns you again with God's blessing.

It is interesting to note that *stumbling* and *offence* are two words that are often interchanged or interconnected throughout scripture. Jesus was called *"A stone of stumbling and a rock of offence"*[2].

To be offended is to literally stumble in your walk; it leaves you flat on the ground and wounded.

And even if you are in the right, which is often the case, we are never justified in holding offence at someone. In essence, it is an expression of faithlessness that God will deal justly and protect us. Jesus once said, *"God will bring justice quickly, but will He find faith in the mean time?"*[3]

When we take the position of judge on the actions of a person, even if it is the inner vow of a wounded young child, we often block God from dealing with that person, and always block access to God's grace in our own life. If we position ourselves as the judge, then we are doing God's job for Him. This may even result in God taking the position of that person's defender, since we are their accuser!

We cannot transform ourselves, that is God's job. But we are responsible for the way we think, and how we form the inner vows by which we live. Romans 12:2 teaches that we are transformed by renewing our mind. By changing our thinking, we open ourselves up to receiving the fullness of God's will and blessing in our lives.

The only victim of our judgments is ourselves. Offence is not a right, it is a childish lack of faith in God. Our judgments are an attempt at making another person pay for their sin through our personal response, be it inward or outward.

Offence is a way of thinking that needs to be repented of. It is a result of believing the lie that I am responsible for correcting, addressing or penalising the bad decisions of another person.

There is only one way to deal with the offence caused by another person's actions – we clear the scales of justice.

You may be familiar with the icon of many law courts – the statue representing blind justice. In it we see a blindfolded woman holding scales in balance. It infers that retribution must match the crime.

But in the kingdom, we must leave God to be that judge. He alone must hold the scales – not blindfolded, but with eyes open to all the facts and pre-conditions. When we hold them, we feel obliged to keep the scales in balance. We want to pay back in proportion to our hurt – to react to the pain that has been caused.

But today's passage in Matthew 18 is clear. We must wipe the scales clear of the weight we hold against people. We must repent by declaring to the spiritual realm, *"I leave this person clear of my offence – I hold no weight against them. I leave them in the hands of God who judges justly"*.

We do that while keeping in mind the size of our own debt that has been forgiven.

A life of forgiveness is fundamental in facilitating personal transformation. Without it we are locked down, unable to move on or grow. You were made for better than that. Do not let the actions of someone else rob you of freedom and hold you as an eternal victim.

PRAYER

Lord, when I consider the issues that keep me locked down and bitter, will you help me see if there is an inner vow or judgment that is in opposition to your will?

Who do I need to forgive, Lord?

REFERENCES

1. Mark 6:3–5
2. 1 Peter 2:8
3. Luke 18:8 (paraphrased)

YOUR RESPONSE

What has held you back in life, or been the point of restricted blessing? When you asked God, who did He say that you need to forgive? Why would that be? What inner vow might have resulted from your judgments of another? Are there people or situations you now avoid, or a life path you chose out of spite or rebellion?

_____

_____

_____

_____

_____

_____

_____

_____

_____

_____

_____

_____

Navigating a turn

Read First: 1 Kings 19

Elijah loved and served God. He had literally put his whole life on the line for God's purposes and people. He had shown incredible courage and a great deal of faith in ridding the land of evil practices and people.

But the Elijah we see in 1 Kings 19 was tired. He was also somewhat depressed and fearful.

In his exhausted state, Elijah's faith and godly thinking had deserted him. He saw himself as alone and worthless. As such, Elijah could think of nothing better than to die.

See how the combination of vulnerability and wrong thinking can skew reality. This was the same man who had just slain hundreds. God was still the same God who had given Elijah great power and who had delivered him over the last couple of days.

And so God took it upon himself to restore Elijah's heart and calling. He gave Elijah a *kairos* moment on his flight into the desert as he rested, giving him grace in the form of food and encouragement.

It was a gentle reality check. Elijah was not alone and worthless. God was still God, and He was with Elijah in his darkest moment.

God met him again at the end of that journey as Elijah dwelt on Horeb. It was the "mountain of fire", the place where God had originally called Moses and later gave the Ten Commandments. This was no ordinary mountain; it was the place of divine calling.

There God spoke to Elijah, getting him to repent of the way he was thinking about life, himself, and about God. God exchanged Elijah's fears with love – providing food and confirming his calling to impact the nation.

Repentance requires more than a *kairos* moment. It is not enough to identify where we are going wrong. We need an alternative to press in to. We turn away from one way of thinking and turn in to another.

We do that best when we have a plan of some sort. Part of God's restoration for Elijah was to give him that plan. He told him what to do and who to do it with. The plan would give surety to Elijah's thinking, ensuring that when doubts and fears came again he had a clear path to follow.

The fears that hounded Elijah pursue many of us as well. In fact, fear is another major slave driver that results in us bowing to an idol. And that idol is called Control.

Elijah feared people like Jezebel. He feared redundancy because his job had seemed futile. He feared aloneness as he presumed it was only him who followed God. And so he took control of things, albeit in a self-destructive way.

But don't we all do that at some point?

We fear the future, wondering if we will have enough to be comfortable. We fear what people think of us lest we become despised or devalued. We fear death and sickness, believing that God could never give us the grace to endure.

And so we take control of our life, deferring to our idol rather than engaging more deeply with God. We forget the truth that:

> *There is no fear in love. But perfect love drives out fear, because fear has to do with punishment. The one who fears is not made perfect in love.*[1]

As we see in Elijah's story, we need the help of a simple strategy if we are to navigate the turn away from our wrong thinking. In those *kairos* moments, when we recognise our fear, anger, desires and judgments, it isn't enough to merely acknowledge that there is a problem.

If you attempt to simply out-run your fears, or eternally "not go there" with your judgment of others, one day your exhaustion will ensure your capture.

You need a place to run to, as much as you need clarity on what to run from. God did not just tell Elijah that he was wrong in his thinking, He showed him a way forward.

Elijah's *kairos* moment was obvious – he was depressed and fearful, tired of living. God met him right where he was at, despite the fact that he had never been further from God's call on his life.

God then gently worked on Elijah to show up his wrong thinking. First, there was some repentance to be done. Elijah had assumed it was just him, and that his work was all in vain now that Jezebel had put a contract on his life. But God clarified the situation, informing Elijah that there were thousands out there who followed God's cause.

God even pressed the point further by revealing Himself within the gentleness of a whisper. Elijah was used to fire and brimstone; it was the hallmark of his ministry so far. But now God was engaging him in a new way for a new day. Elijah's work was to be subtler now – more precise in its outworking.

Only then was Elijah ready to plan a way forward. To navigate the turn, he needed to know where to turn to. He needed a preferred future – a dream worth aiming for.

And so God spelled out for Elijah in some detail the way to bring about this grander vision. There were routes to traverse and people to anoint.

This was enough to give Elijah hope. And it is hope that energises us to move forward. Without hope, our hearts decay and stagnate.

> *Hope deferred makes the heart sick, but*
> *a longing fulfilled is a tree of life.*[2]

What then will you be turning towards?

Earlier in the book, in chapter 2.6, you were asked to determine your unacceptable present, and a preferred future. Now that you have processed a little more about where you might need to repent, look again at those answers.

Where do you need to turn from, and what do need to turn towards? Jesus often said that repentance has its own fruit[3] – what might your fruit be if repentance and belief were to do their work in you?

How will you begin to navigate a turn?

PRAYER

Lord, I will not be able to change much of anything unless you help me. As I consider where an alternate direction for me might be, will you show what has produced the bad fruit that requires repentance.

Show me too what it would look like to have a more abundant life as you promise me. I want to take the steps of faith and hope towards your calling. I trust in accordance with 2 Peter 1:3 that your divine power has given me everything I need for a godly life through my knowledge of you who called me by your own glory and goodness.

Amen.

REFERENCES

1. 1 John 4:18
2. Proverbs 13:12
3. Mark 3:8; Luke 3:8

YOUR RESPONSE

When determining a preferred future, you do not yet need to know fully how to get there. You can assume that you will need the help of God and His people to go forward. For now, you need to be clear about what thoughts, fears, judgments and inner vows you may need to turn from – and what you want to replace them with.

What will you turn from, and where will you turn to?

Group Session 5

INTRODUCTION

This week you have spent time and prayer seeking God for some underlying issues in your life. We all have these dark closets, some of which we didn't even know existed. Some of us have simply thought the closet to be irrelevant or inevitable, and so it has remained taking up space in our life.

The only reason we open those doors is to shine a light and bring redemption. Introspection is something that should be measured and done with a heart to bring change, not sadness.

Q. What was your overall response to the week of teaching on repentance?

YOUR RESPONSES FROM THE PAST WEEK

Have you carried a residual load in the form of the burden of brokenness or sin? Share your response to chapter 4.1.

4.1 Where have you experienced spiritual tiredness? What have been the struggles you are unable to overcome in your own strength?

Repentance begins with turning away from a form of thinking or behaving. What conclusions did you come to when you sought God for the reasons behind the dysfunction you want to address? Share your responses to chapters 4.2 and 4.3.

4.2 In regard to the issue you have chosen to address, what might be the wrong thinking that has led to that being a long-standing part of your life?

What lies might you believe about yourself, or about God? Where do you need to turn your thinking?

4.3 In chapter 1.4 you identified an idol that you bow to. What is it? Why do you think it has come to have the place in your life that it does? Is there a lie you have believed and need to repent of?

Some key issues were raised in this week's content that contribute to many of our broken ways of living:

1. **Orphaned spirit:** A disengaged heart that seeks intimacy, provision and identity apart from God.

2. **Dishonour:** Not valuing the people that God has placed as a source of blessing in our life.

3. **Unforgiveness:** Forming a judgment and holding an offence.

4. **Inner vows:** In response to the imperfect environment we find ourselves in as a child, we determine to go on a foolish path that takes control of our destiny.

Share your responses and subsequent processing of these issue in your life from chapters 4.4 and 4.5.

4.4 Perhaps the issue of dishonour is not one that you need to consider. If you have prayed and feel that you hold everyone in the level of regard that God expects, then enjoy the rewards of that. However, if God has raised an issue for you to deal with, write it down here, and include your prayerful response in how to deal with it.

4.5 What has held you back in life or been the point of restricted blessing? When you asked God, who did He say that you need to forgive? Why would that be? What inner vow might have resulted from your judgments of another? Are there people or situations you now avoid, or a life path you chose out of spite or rebellion?

What might your alternative future look like in regard to these issues? What will you turn to? Share your response from chapter 4.6.

4.6 When determining a preferred future, you do not yet need to know fully how to get there. You can assume that you will need the help of God and His people to go forward. For now, you need to be clear about what thoughts, fears, judgments and inner vows you may need to turn from – and what you want to replace them with.

What will you turn from, and where will you turn to?

WHERE TO FROM HERE?

You need God's grace to overcome. We are not designed to live or grow in our own strength; that is why you have found it impossible up until now.

The next week of readings invite you into a journey of faith where you can posture yourself to grasp the elements of kingdom life that meet your needs.

Pray together that each participant will be able to receive the particular grace God has for them.

5.1

The kingdom at hand

READ FIRST: HEBREWS 11

Faith.

It is one of the least understood dynamics of our spiritual life.

Some say faith is believing for what we do not yet have. But that more accurately describes hope, since hope is always based in a potential future, not what we already possess[1].

Faith is a reliance on what we do already have – sometimes it is visible, sometimes it is not.

Where faith and hope coexist is when God has promised us something for our future that we do not yet possess. But our faith is not in the future that we do not have; it is in the promise that we do have. We might more correctly say that our faith is in the Promise-giver. God is always true, and so what He promises is also sure.

At its core, faith is all about active reliance.

You might assume that a chair can hold up your weight, but you do not actually exercise faith until you commit yourself to sitting on it. Biblical faith is always more than a way of thinking; it has an action that fulfils the rationale.

In regards to the rhythm of grace we are focusing on in this material – that of repentance and belief – we have come to the point where we must learn how to apply faith in the process of transformation towards spiritual empowerment.

Our anchor verse to explain this dynamic is Mark 1:15, in which Jesus says:

> *"The time has come," he said. "The kingdom of God has come near. Repent and believe the good news!"*

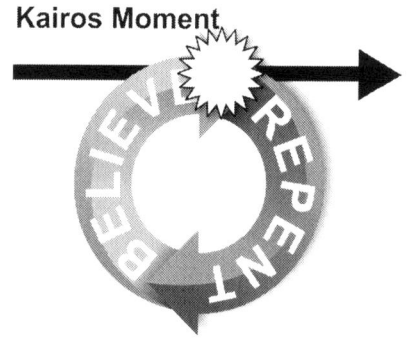

We have already identified what your *kairos* times can look like as we journey along our normal day. We have also looked at repentance – understanding what to turn from, and what to turn to.

Now we consider belief, or faith. How are we to rely on God to do what we have so often failed to do in our own strength?

First, we should ensure our faith is only in what God has provided, or has promised to provide.

He has not, for example, promised us that the world would go easy on us, or that He will remove our choice or desire to do evil. He has not promised that life would always make sense, or that we would understand why things don't always work out the way we think they should.

We can, however, always have faith in what we do possess through the blood of Christ. We can trust in His promise that:

> *His divine power has given us everything we need for a godly life through our knowledge of him who called us by his own glory and goodness.[2]*

We can rely on that. We have the power within us through God's Spirit to overcome and choose God's way in every situation. That is indeed good news!

How we access that power is the big question. Most of us know it is there, but fewer are equipped to walk in it.

A clue lies in the way Jesus pre-empted the rhythm of grace we are studying. He said, *"the kingdom of God is near"*.

The inference is that we can reach out and grasp this kingdom since it is at hand. In some way the king's domain (king-dom) can be applied to our lives. And whatever those elements of the kingdom might be, we can have faith in them and the great God behind them. We know that they will be sufficient to fulfil what God wants us to fulfil.

So, how does this work in practice?

We know that the dynamic we have committed to involves us turning from an old way of thinking and acting and turning towards something better. We also know that we cannot change on our own. We need God's grace to give us what cannot give ourselves.

That grace is found in the kingdom of God – which is why Jesus implored people to seek a life within that kingdom[3].

Elsewhere He said that the kingdom is found within us[4]. It is not a place or a lifestyle ... the kingdom is a state of heart where God reigns over every part.

The kingdom is a place of absolute faith. It is the existence of shalom: perfect peace between God, people and the planet. The apostle Paul put it this way:

*For the kingdom of God is not a matter of
eating and drinking, but of righteousness,
peace and joy in the Holy Spirit.*[5]

Take a moment to read that again.

Paul is confirming that the kingdom is a state of heart where God reigns. And where He is sovereign of all, there is righteousness, peace and joy.

Here is the point. If you want to experience the power of God in your life to do all the things scripture promises, then your heart needs to dwell in this perfect peace. It is in that place where we connect most powerfully with God.

Think of it. In shalom there is no fear. In God's presence there is no striving or discord. When we are dwelling in His perfect love, we need no other thing. The world cannot give this peace and, more importantly, it cannot take it away.

The power to overcome your past and determine your present reality is found through experiencing the kingdom. We turn from fear and embrace the reality of God's love. We can turn away from bitterness and judgment and have faith in God's justice.

In regard to our desires that lead to death, we can ask God about the real needs we are trying to have met, and turn to His design instead.

In the kingdom, all is righteous. That refers to right standing. Righteousness means that things are as they should be when God is King. There is forgiveness, healing, perfection and peace.

Find the kingdom, and you find faith. Find faith, and God's Spirit does the rest.

PRAYER

Today Lord, I declare with the Psalmist who longs to be in your presence ...

> Who may ascend the mountain of the LORD?
> Who may stand in his holy place? The one who
> has clean hands and a pure heart, who does not
> trust in an idol or swear by a false god.

> They will receive blessing from the LORD and vindication
> from God their Savior. Such is the generation of those
> who seek him, who seek your face, God of Jacob.

> Lift up your heads, you gates; be lifted up, you ancient
> doors, that the King of glory may come in. Who is this King
> of glory? The LORD strong and mighty, the LORD mighty
> in battle. Lift up your heads, you gates; lift them up, you
> ancient doors, that the King of glory may come in.

Who is he, this King of glory? The LORD Almighty—
he is the King of glory. (Psalm 24:1–10)

REFERENCES

1. Romans 8:24–25
2. 2 Peter 1:3
3. Matthew 6:33
4. Luke 17:21
5. Romans 14:17

YOUR RESPONSE

Considering the issue in which you want transformation, what element of the kingdom do you need to embrace? What grace do you need from God?

_____

_____

_____

_____

_____

_____

_____

What storm?

God's primary agenda is not to improve the circumstances of your life – but for you to find life.

God does not promise that things will go well for us – but He has made a way for it to be well with our soul.

Jesus did not offer us better circumstances – but He does offer us to live above those circumstances.

"Hey Jesus, we are in a four-metre boat and there is a five-metre swell. We are drenched and cold, and I don't think we are going to make it. Have you noticed?"

"No, I was asleep. Didn't you notice that?"

Jesus didn't acknowledge weather conditions as an indicator of safety. Therefore, He didn't take them into account. He drew no connection between circumstance and well-being.

When it comes to contemplating or applying change to our life, we often hope for a break in the traffic. If life would just pause for a moment, we could take stock, pray and apply a new idea. Then we could re-engage with our hectic world fully prepared.

But life rarely does that. The demands do not cease. The temptation, anger and frustration just keep coming. The babies keep crying, the phone never stops, workmates keep slandering and swearing, the boss keeps demanding, and the economy continues to threaten our career.

The storms keep thrashing against the fisherman's boat. And yet Jesus sleeps.

What is more, He assumes that you would too. *"Why are you so afraid? Do you still have no faith?"*[1]

Faith in what?

Should we have faith that Jesus will calm the seas? We can if He has promised as much. But what if He has not? I think Jesus' point is deeper than that.

What happens when we have no direct promise to lean on? In those strategic seasons where God is stretching our faith and developing character in us, He might deliberately stay quiet on an issue. But why would He do that?

He does it so that we will lean in to Him, not a formula or circumstance. He wants us to find our faith in Himself, not just a promise. True spirituality is about direct and intimate relationship with God.

Sure, faith in what God says, and what He has said, is a fundamental and sound part of Christian life. But deeper and more meaningful again is faith in who God is. His goodness knows no bounds. His love motivates all he does. He is faithful and true. We rely primarily on who He is, not what He does or doesn't do.

> *And so we know and rely on the love*
> *God has for us. God is love.*[2]

This is what it means to find ourselves in Him. The appreciation of our personal value, the definition of our purpose, even our perspective on physical safety are sourced from our faith in who God is.

No matter what is going on around us, we are expected to have faith in God – we lean on and rely on Him.

In that posture we can receive all we need – the strength, the encouragement, the wisdom and peace.

Once that issue is settled, and only then, do some more interesting dynamics open up.

Jesus didn't need the storm to be settled, but He settled it anyway. The same faith that allowed Him to sleep in the storm brought the authority for Him to quell it. Because Jesus was not a slave to the weather, He was free to overrule it.

We only have authority over the storms we can sleep through.

If we are afraid of poverty, or require success at our workplace to find our significance, we will never have spiritual authority in that setting. Romans 6:16 says we are slaves to whatever we obey. Likewise, if you need the approval of others, you will never be able to make a moral stand in their midst. This carries over into every area of our life.

If you need to gain authority over any area, you need to position your heart so that the issue doesn't own you.

Jesus could calm the storm because there was no storm within Him. Where He dwelt, there were no storms, just the love of the Father.

A friend of mine was working through this very issue when his wife, 24 weeks pregnant, had her waters break. It was way too early, but the baby was coming. Their previous child was born with a degree of abnormality so they had some grounds for concern that this was not going to end well at all.

As they were on their way to the hospital in the ambulance, I called. The paramedics confirmed that the fluids had drained out and the baby had to come in the next day.

"How are you guys doing?" I asked.

"Sleeping through the storm", came the reply. Instantly, faith was activated in all of us. Authority over the storm was available, it was time to act! And so we went to prayer.

When she got to the hospital, the doctors confirmed the situation and placed the mother in the ward ready to deliver the baby. But the baby didn't come.

After some hours they re-examined the situation and found to their amazement that the womb was fully sealed and the amniotic fluids in place as if nothing had happened!

That baby ended up coming in to the world a couple of weeks late, and in perfect health.

Authority is only found when we are not slaves to circumstance.

This is the faith that transforms us.

We find God most powerfully when we come to Him in peace. Our needs are met most profoundly when we acknowledge that we need only Him.

We are only free to overcome the world when we no longer need it.

PRAYER

Lord, what are the storms in my life that I have let overrule my heart?

Help me today to look at them from the perspective of heaven. Help me to find rest in my soul, knowing that, whatever comes, I always have you.

Today I choose to worship from that place.

Amen

REFERENCES

1. Mark 4:40
2. 1 John 4:16

YOUR RESPONSE

Has there been a situation or circumstance that, until now, you have seen as the reason why you cannot break through? How does this idea of peace in the storm apply to your life?

_____

_____

_____

_____

_____

The rest of faith

"How could God allow that to happen to me?"

"If God would just do this, I would know He is real and interested in me."

"Because of the things done to me, I cannot find peace in my heart."

Have you ever said or heard any of these statements? They are the statements of an orphaned spirit – a state of heart that feels alone and afraid.

They are also statements of a heart that somewhat objectifies God. The relationship is based more in function than faith. It assumes a cause and effect system where if we do this then God must do that.

That is what it looks like when we have made God an idol. By breaking the first commandment to have no god before Him, we naturally break the second commandment and turn to a detached idol we want to do something for us.

In honesty, however, the alternative can seem a little like jumping off a cliff.

That alternative is to surrender all to this God we cannot see, regardless of what has or will happen to us.

That is faith.

Perhaps we could call it spiritual free-fall.

It is an attitude that believes God meets my deepest needs – the ones that matter more than my past, the injustices that take place routinely, and the things I would love to see happen in my life.

It is faith in the middle of a stormy sea. It is rest in the midst of relentless obligations. It is identity and security regardless of performance or appearance. It is shalom.

God makes for a lousy idol.

If you expect Him to do what you want, or calm the endless turbulence of life, you will be a frustrated and disappointed person. He does not serve us nor does He promise to make your life comfortable.

"Trouble is coming", Jesus would say. *"I don't like it, and I didn't design it. But it is coming because this world is broken. But take heart, I am bigger than all this. And I am in you."*[1]

Once, when I was a young man, I sat talking to God about my life. I had finally realised that I could not live up to anything like the standards I read about in scripture. I was, of course, just owning up to the obvious.

But I came in the posture of spiritual free-fall.

"I cannot live this life without your help. But I am committed anyway, even if I continue to fail miserably."

What happened next has become something of a pattern, both in my life and in those I disciple.

As I surrendered my life, regardless of the cost, God tangibly and powerfully filled me with His Spirit in a whole new way. My head lifted and I began talking to God in a language I had never heard. I know now He had released in me the gift of languages, a way to bypass my mind so I could pray to Him, spirit-to-Spirit. This despite the fact that back then I didn't even believe the gift existed.

God had anointed me with the power I needed to live the season of life I was in.

Over the years I have had many such experiences, all unique, and all resulting from a new surrender in a new season. At times He allows me to experience a tangible manifestation of His love. At others, He has anointed me with the power to minister supernaturally to others in a new way.

He knows what we need and when we need it. That is His job and that is His prerogative.

Our role is to surrender totally and seek to live in peace. That peace is most easily found when we, in total faith, lift off ourselves the need to understand the seeming inconsistencies and hardships of our walk with God.

Peace is best found through life's storms when I do not allow the things I don't understand to rob me of what I do understand.

If I need God to do something for me before I find rest, or if I need it all to make sense before I trust, then I will never know supernatural peace. What He offers is a peace that is beyond understanding. It is not of the mind, but of the spirit.

*Do not be anxious about anything, but in
every situation, by prayer and petition, with
thanksgiving, present your requests to God.*

*And the peace of God, which transcends all understanding,
will guard your hearts and your minds in Christ Jesus.[2]*

We find God most powerfully when we look for Him in a state of peace. If we are fearful and desperate, we will struggle to hear His voice. If we are insecure and ashamed, we won't be able to discern His reassurance of value. If we want to tell

Him that life is hopeless, He will not engage since He does not agree with you.

We meet God most profoundly when we do so on His terms.

Romans 14:17 defines the kingdom of God in terms of righteousness, peace and joy. Those three elements present a sequence that delivers a powerful and overcoming life.

Righteousness is a state of right-standing. It means we are able to stand before God, naked and unashamed. He sees us through the lens of His Son – eyes wide open and fully embracing of us.

That righteousness gives us access to peace. Our unconditional security, significance and identity allow us to rest in who we are, thanks to who God is.

Righteousness and peace, once truly experienced, result in an inevitable joy that is beyond the turbulence of our broken life.

It doesn't matter what is wrong. It doesn't matter what makes sense. All that matters is the eternal reality of our life with God.

This is the rest of faith. God is good, He is enough, and He is for you. With that perspective you will begin to walk in step with the Spirit, aware that it is His power that drives you forward.

PRAYER

Lord, have I put conditions on my surrender to you? Have I been holding back from total surrender and adoration? Show me what stands between me and the faith of free-fall. Give me the grace to jump in to your safe hand.

Amen.

REFERENCES

1. 1 John 16:33; 1 John 4:4 (My paraphrase)
2. Philippians 4:6–7

YOUR RESPONSE

What is stopping you from finding peace with God? Is there a prayer that remains unanswered? A situation you expect Him to fix? Will you surrender to God in faith, not needing those things to be solved?

Spend a few minutes now writing out a prayer of surrender to God.

_____

_____

_____

_____

5.4

Pathway to joy

READ FIRST: PSALM 100:1–4

If you were to follow the threads of purpose that guide so much of our ambitions and desires, you would be surprised where they lead.

Why do we try so hard to get what we are after? Whether it be good looks, material possessions, financial security, great relationships ... or even instant gratification, we are looking for something.

That something could be called peace. And by that I mean a form of settledness that comes from all our inner tensions finding resolution. This is what we were always designed for, and it was what humanity experienced in Eden before the fall.

This sort of peace – that which the Hebrews called Shalom – produced an interesting fruit.

Joy.

We are wired to live in joy. Over the last few chapters we have kept coming back to Romans 14:17 which says that the kingdom of God is defined as righteousness, then peace, and ultimately joy – found in the Holy Spirit.

The reason why this is such an intrinsic part of the journey to transforming our brokenness is that fundamentally we are beginning to change the focus, source and definition of our joy.

Joy is what we want, but depending on where we believe it comes from, and what we think joy looks like, the paths we choose will be very different.

For an emotionally and spiritually healthy Christian, that joy comes from the Holy Spirit. It is a fruit produced from God's active presence in our life. To engage with the Spirit at that level, our thought life needs to be aligned with the kingdom way of thinking.

Joy requires us to have settled assurance that I do not need life to look a certain way to know peace. It is confidence that I will always ultimately be secure in God's love and presence, whether I live or die.

As we apply Jesus' rhythm of grace of Repent and Believe, it is our belief in God as the fulfilment of our joy that holds the key.

God, knowing we are creatures of habit, has provided a repeatable pathway to joy. He has made this pathway to help form our minds and our hearts in a way that joy is inevitable. In some ways this pathway replicates in our hearts what was at one time visible to the Hebrews – the architecture of the temple.

The Hebrew temple was the place where God's presence dwelt. To get in to the most holy place, you had to pass through a gate, then through an open courtyard and finally into the sanctuary behind the curtain. It was quite a ritual and one full of symbolism. And yet Psalm 100 shows us how to apply that same sequence in our personal journey to engaging God's powerful presence.

In verse four we start by acknowledging that God is indeed Lord and Protector of our life. This is important. If we believe a lie about who God is, we will not embrace the full blessings that come from who He really is.

We are then commissioned to enter His gates with thanksgiving.

When we thank God, we are recognising and appreciating His works. By celebrating His beautiful deeds, we begin to align our thinking more clearly with truth. When we focus on what He has done, we remember more clearly His goodness and majesty.

Thanksgiving also takes our minds away from the frustration that comes from what we might think God hasn't done. Our in-built sense of entitlement tends to place expectations on God to do this or that, and our disappointment leads us down a mental track that brings unnecessary disillusionment.

Acknowledging God's works, however, is just skimming the atmosphere in this process. His works tell us about His ways. His works are an invitation to go deeper – to look at the source of such goodness and power.

And so we enter His courts with praise. That praise is connected to God's nature – we are celebrating who He is, not just what He has done. Praise makes it more personal; it is a choice for one personality to honour another personality fully.

In the ancient days, the Hebrews would bring a sacrifice in to the courts. This was a symbol of the One who was to come and die in our place so we could be reconciled to God.

Now however, our sacrifice is praise!

Let us continually offer to God a sacrifice of praise—
the fruit of lips that openly profess his name.[1]

A sacrifice is costly, that is the whole point. It is appropriate that our praise to God goes beyond what is convenient or comfortable. We should shout about His goodness and physically lift our hands, even bowing to the ground when appropriate. The idea of stoic and conservative expressions of praise are hard to find in scripture, and it can be hard to rationalise in practice.

There is one final step to go – literally into God's presence. This is most readily done through true and proper worship. Worship is a relational act, one where we lift up One who is worthy.

In worship, the sacrifice is us.

All of us. Our plans, our priorities and our perceived right to control our destiny.

> *Therefore, I urge you, brothers and sisters, in view of God's mercy, to offer your bodies as a living sacrifice, holy and pleasing to God—this is your true and proper worship.[2]*

Worship that is not "true and proper" is not acceptable worship. We are not to bring our words in the absence of our hearts.

This form of worship, where we offer God our whole lives, is another way to describe surrender.

This is the pathway to joy.

To cut off the entanglements of the world and simply offer ourselves to God regardless of consequence.

This is also the pathway to true transformation, since it is the ultimate expression of belief.

And we all, who with unveiled faces contemplate the Lord's glory, are being transformed into his image with ever-increasing glory, which comes from the Lord, who is the Spirit.[3]

PRAYER

Lord, today I come before you with all the conditions removed. I just want you, and nothing else. You are the true Source of joy, and it is you I want to dwell with forever. Help me to worship you with my whole heart, soul, strength and mind – and as I contemplate your glory, transform me into your image more clearly.

Amen.

REFERENCES

1. Hebrews 13:15
2. Romans 12:1
3. 2 Corinthians 3:18

YOUR RESPONSE

What has been the source of your joy to this point? When has the Lord provided you with the deepest sense of His joy in your life?

_____

_____

_____

_____

_____

_____

_____

_____

_____

_____

_____

_____

_____

_____

5.5

The higher calling

READ FIRST: 1 CHRONICLES 4:9–10

Jabez longed for more from his life than the cards he had been dealt would allow.

His name literally meant *pain*. He was given birth in pain, and he had continued to live in pain. Whether the discomfort he experienced was physical, emotional, relational or circumstantial, we will never know.

It doesn't matter what the problem was, what mattered, according to scripture, is that he was honourable in that situation. Now, there is a word we do not hear much of – *honour*. Back then it meant that you lived your life in such a way that people automatically held your parents in high regard. Your excellence and wisdom would be such that people would assume your parents had done a marvelous job on you.

And even though he started at the back of the field, Jabez went for first prize.

All we know is that his famous prayer was one that drew the admiration of heaven: *"Bless me and enlarge my territory – be with me so I will no longer be a pain!"*[1]

It is safe to assume that God answered that prayer.

Did you realise that you too have an incredible first prize available?

But that prize is not one you can have access to, or even see, until you have determined in your heart that living the spirit-empowered life is the only option for you. This is a unique and amazing dynamic of Christian life.

Allow me to explain.

In as much as an individual determines to lower their expectations of character, calling and spiritual living to that of the world around them, they are blind to the vibrancy of the future on offer from God. It's like they have deeply tinted glasses on, filtering out the fullness of life's colour.

By engaging fully with God's Spirit, you remove the lenses, accessing the fullness of who you are in Him. Until that moment, you are living a half-life. You are dust without breath. And the New Testament draws a clear line between those who live by the spirit and those who don't[2].

Those who do not live by the Spirit are regarded as spiritual slaves to their old nature. Those who do are categorised as children or, more importantly, as sons. This is a non-gender term that relates to our position in God's household. Sons are those who have come of age and are mature enough to take on the family business. They are ready to manage and grow the inheritance.

> *Because you are his sons, God sent the Spirit of his Son into our hearts, the Spirit who calls out, "Abba, Father". So you are no longer a slave, but God's child; and since you are his child, God has made you also an heir.[3]*

People sometimes struggle to form a preferred future for themselves that is magnificent enough to motivate them out of their sin and brokenness. They might say, *"I can see God wants me to live a different way, but the situation I am in is tolerable, why would I give it up?"*

The inheritance on offer is unknown and remains unknowable until the Spirit more fully controls their life and determines their vision. They can see what they need to turn from but not what they are to turn to.

It is not until there is a radical step of belief in God, usually one that follows repentance, that the world begins to look very different. It is like a veil comes off their life, similar to what Paul described when he said:

*But whenever anyone turns to the Lord, the veil is
taken away. Now the Lord is the Spirit, and where
the Spirit of the Lord is, there is freedom[4].*

Jabez had turned to the Lord, refusing to be defined
anymore by his past. In doing so he opened up access to
an increased inheritance. He used the same terms that we
see Paul later using to refer to his God-assigned field of
influence, or territory[5].

God has an inheritance for you. It relates to His very own
family business, the kingdom of God.

Without the Spirit, we become enamoured with building
our own empire. But God refuses to empower empires, He is
only into the kingdom. Jesus could have taken over Rome, the
greatest empire the world had seen, but instead He scorned
it. The kingdom of God is so much grander.

You have an assigned boundary of influence. God's Spirit
gives you the grace required to steward and even grow that
influence as you mature even more.

But as long as you are committed to your own empire, you
will not see it. The inheritance remains veiled.

Your empire may be as small as your own tendency to
prop up insecurities or avoid fears, or it may be as large as a
self-made millionaire's fortune. It doesn't matter. If you seek
to build anything but God's kingdom in God's way, it will all
blow away to dust[6].

Your inheritance is related to the people God has placed you amongst. Your family, your church, your workplace and your city. They are your field. For them to flourish as they should will require you to take your place, fully engaged with them, and be compelled by the Spirit.

There is no joy like that of being fully engaged with God's purposes in this way.

Knowing that the work you do down here will matter for eternity is a profound privilege.

If you were to take a moment to consider all the people and positions that the world views as worthy of esteem or celebrity, how would they stack up against God's eternal purpose?

And yet you are free to dream with God about how to influence your field of inheritance. Every single aspect of that gets credited to your account in heaven, building up your rewards of faithfulness.

You might personally impact the world for the kingdom. Or, what you do may influence one or many who go on to influence thousands.

Regardless of the size and shape of your field, what matters is that it counts for a lot, and counts for eternity. Only that which is done for God's kingdom will last forever.

Are you ready to give up your empire in order to embrace your inheritance in the kingdom?

PRAYER

Lord, as I continue to say yes to your call to surrender, I pray that you would bless me. As you did with Jabez, increase my territory and expand my influence for your glory.

Give me dreams of what can be, and plans for what should be.

Amen.

REFERENCES

1. 1 Chronicles 4:10
2. Romans 8:14–17; Galatians 4:1–7
3. Galatians 4:6–7
4. 2 Corinthians 3:16–17
5. 2 Corinthians 10:13–16
6. 1 Corinthians 3:12–15

YOUR RESPONSE

Where has God placed you that requires you to steward that inheritance? Are there people in your family, community or workplace that need you to cover them in prayer? How could you focus better on growing God's family business?

A point of no return

READ FIRST: GENESIS 22:1–18

Abraham had always thought that Isaac was the fulfilment of his calling to bless the nations. Always aware of his higher calling, Abraham lived to see Isaac born.

For 25 years he had waited for God to fulfil His promise to bring forth nations from Abraham. Often, however, the wait had gone beyond a joke for him and his wife Sarah. They had battled their attitude and confusion constantly, eventually reverting to a Plan B of sorts. They had gone about things on their own initiative and come up with Ishmael, a son born to Abraham's maidservant.

Ishmael, a very real person, was born from a failure of faith. And unknown to Abraham, it was faith that was supposed to be the blessing he brought to the world.

Eventually their son Isaac was indeed born, and it must have seemed like the end of the challenge for Abraham. That is, until God called him out one more time and instructed him to sacrifice his son.

It must have seemed a barbaric and unthinkable request, and yet he proceeded on the journey without hesitation.

He did not understand what was going on, and that was the point. We do not need too much faith when everything makes sense and we have an idea what God is planning for our life. But when the messages seem mixed, the guidance is ambiguous or absent, and the spiritual signposts are conflicting, it is then that real faith is needed.

Faith is at its best when we do not understand everything.

Faith takes that which we do know for sure and banks everything on that, in the midst of many other unanswered questions. Faith ensures that what we do not understand can't rob us of what we do understand.

Abraham had learned the hard way that God is faithful and powerful to fulfil His word. So He relied on that, believing that God would raise Isaac from the dead[1].

When it comes to us surrendering to God in faith, it can seem like we are standing at the edge of a cliff. As the chasm claws at us from below, we know that there is no surviving the fall unless God Himself catches us. But, like Abraham, we know that there is no going back – life at the top of the cliff is no longer acceptable.

And so it is forward we go, unsure of how it will end, but sure that God's hand will be outstretched.

What would that jump translate to being in your situation?

Someone bound up with fear of man might need to confront the person who seems to control their fate. The addicted person might need to cut off all possibility of access to their harmful supply. The wounded heart might need to demonstrate forgiveness of the unrepentant one who hurt them.

Such decisions feel like plunging off a thousand metre drop. Survival seems impossible.

And yet, God catches us. Not so soon that the jump isn't committed to, but soon enough that we are safe. His hand is a couple of metres down. Yes, even that fall might leave you with a scratch or two, but nothing permanent – nothing that scars.

The journeys God calls us on in faith are not absent of pain altogether. Can you imagine the soul-tearing images that would have filled Abraham's mind as he took the three-day walk to Moriah with Isaac?

This type of internal stress in itself can become enough to cause great anguish, even before anything has actually happened. Often the thought of something happening is worse than the reality.

Engineers have an interesting way to define stress which differs from a lay-person's understanding. We see stress as an external force pressing in on us, but physics would describe it differently. In reality, the external forces applied are called *strain*. The internal resistance to that strain is called *stress*.

Stress is our personal response to an external pressure, whether it be real or perceived. We get to choose how we respond internally – we actually have control over the stress we feel. If we try to resist with the strength we have, then we might not be able to sustain it. But if we defer that load into God's hands, refusing to bear the burden ourselves, then we survive.

When we choose to delegate the burden in this way, it is possible to flourish in the midst of unthinkable hardship. We only suffer when we feel responsible to resist the strain alone.

Relying on God is the purest definition of a life of faith.

It is an ongoing choice to rely on God to provide what you never could. Jesus calls us to repent and believe. We turn from self-oriented thinking and self-sustained activity and turn instead to Him for supply.

Faith is the jewel in the crown of life with God and matters more in heaven than almost anything.

For a little while you may have had to suffer grief in all kinds of trials. These have come so that the proven genuineness of your faith—of greater worth than gold, which perishes even though refined by fire—may result in praise, glory and honor when Jesus Christ is revealed.[2]

True steps of faith require us to delete any exit strategy back to our old way of living. Just as a decision to believe in Christ for salvation must be at the exclusion of any other path to God, so our choice to repent and believe must be decisive.

It does not take faith to try and live God's way when there is a backstop waiting in case God "fails". Faith determines that we rely on God fully, or not at all.

Idols must be smashed. Slave drivers must be confronted. Soft options need to be structured out of our lives.

When all such entanglements are removed, we finally discover the peace which grants us access to God's power.

Our small step of faith often begins with us being not fully certain how our feet will fall. But as soon as we commit, we can feel God's strong hand at our back giving strength to go on. We feel too His safe hands beneath our feet holding us up.

Are you ready to take such a step in some area of your life? Abraham, like every believer who has followed, had come to such moments.

Faith, like courage, is not the absence of fear – it is a willingness to commit in the face of it.

PRAYER

Lord, will you show me if there is an area I need to surrender to you? What does my leap of faith look like? What needs to be cut off from my life?

Give me faith today to be your person more fully.

Amen.

REFERENCES

1. Hebrews 11:19
2. 1 Peter 1:6–7

YOUR RESPONSE

If you have come to a point of wanting to proceed in faith with God in a new way, then spend some time now writing a letter of surrender to God. Tell Him where you are committing to alter your life, and in which areas you need His strength and provision. Then offer yourself to Him as an act of worship.

_____

_____

_____

_____

_____

Group Session 6

I wonder if this week's material caught you by surprise. When we consider a life of faith, the conversation normally leans towards themes other than personal surrender and experiencing Shalom!

However, because the kingdom is found by engaging with God's Spirit in humility, faith at its best is found this way.

Q. What was your overall response to this week's content?

_____

YOUR RESPONSES FROM THE PAST WEEK

Read together 2 Peter 1:3–9.

What needs to be added to your life by God for you to transform as you intend? Share together your response to chapter 5.1.

5.1: Considering the issue in which you want transformation – what element of the kingdom do you need to embrace? What grace do you need from God?

Our inner storms take all sorts of shapes and sizes. Often they are the forces that drive our reactions and behaviours. Share together your response to chapter 5.2 and 5.3.

5.1 Has there been a situation or circumstance that, until now, you have seen as the reason why you cannot break through? How does this idea of peace in the storm apply to your life?

5.2 What is stopping you from finding peace with God? Is there a prayer that remains unanswered? A situation you expect Him to fix? Will you surrender to God in faith, not needing those things to be solved?

Spend a few minutes now writing out a prayer of surrender to God.

Christian joy can seem to be a somewhat elusive promise. And yet we all enjoy moments of deep serenity that surpass our circumstances. Share your response to chapter 5.4.

5.3 What has been the source of your joy to this point? When has the Lord provided you with the deepest sense of His joy in your life?

Your life is more about those you influence than it is about you. Your life matters for the sake of your generation and the ones that follow. It takes a degree of maturity to dedicate your strength to an enterprise that is selfless.

Share your response to chapter 5.5.

5.4 Where has God placed you that requires you to steward that inheritance? Are there people in your family, community or workplace that need you to cover them in prayer? How could you focus better on growing God's family business?

Are you at the point of surrender now? If so, read your prayer of surrender from chapter 5.6 to the group. Then pray for each other that God would bless their dedication.

5.5 If you have come to a point of wanting to proceed in faith with God in a new way, then spend some time now writing a letter of surrender to God. Tell Him where you are committing to alter your life, and in which areas you need His strength and provision. Then offer yourself to Him as an act of worship.

What am I aiming for, really?

Some people read James' writings and cringe.

Martin Luther called the book an "Epistle of Straw", and wished it was not in the Bible at all!

It was too binary, Luther thought. Too different to Paul's grand themes of Christ-bought righteousness. Especially when James states that a person is righteous by what they do, not by faith alone[1].

James was indeed quite black and white in his worldview. It was all or nothing for him, and he had proved it. As the brother of Jesus, James had in fact not believed in Jesus at first[2]. But once he did believe, it was all or nothing.

Consider James' journey for a moment.

He was Jesus' younger half-brother, son of Joseph. He would have looked up to his older brother with natural respect. And yet, even with all he witnessed, James still took some convincing. This should give you a little comfort when you feel like your faith is weak. You haven't seen Jesus in the flesh and yet you have placed your faith in Him.

As Jesus said, *"Blessed is the one who believes and yet has not seen"*[3].

So, what did it look like for a guy like James to be "all-in"? How would it look for you, for that matter? Would it be described in terms of holiness, or maybe fruitfulness?

What does first prize look like for those of us who believe in One we don't see, but in whom we place our trust? James summed it up in a confronting way in your reading today.

Do you think Scripture says without reason that he jealously longs for the spirit he has caused to dwell in us?[4]

Amazing! This is what God jealously longs for – your spirit, your heart.

Not for your time, not for your perfection, not for your worship, not for your service. He wants you!

This is the point of pretty much everything in life, both now and for eternity.

Intimacy. Longing. A lover's jealousy.

Anything less than total devotion is seen as adultery in James' mind – and this should rattle us to the core of our being.

God isn't concerned for us looking the part. He condemned those who pursued that line of thinking.

He doesn't want to merely visit you from time to time with some earth-shattering experience. He wants to stay. He wants to join you in powerful habitation, not an infrequent visitation.

He doesn't want to merely give you advice or direction so you can then just turn away and do it. But isn't that what we often reduce the relationship to?

He doesn't want you to struggle with your old nature either; He wants you to kill it. He doesn't want less of you; He wants all of you. He doesn't want you to be perfect; He wants you to be present with Him.

Do you get the message? It isn't about performance at all; God wants your heart. This is first prize in His eyes, and it should be in ours as well.

Why then does God seem so consumed with transforming this heart of ours?

For two reasons. Firstly, it is killing you; and secondly, because your brokenness is getting in the way of your relationship with Him. This was the perspective of James. You can see why he implored us to:

Grieve, mourn and wail. Change your laughter to mourning and your joy to gloom. Humble yourselves before the Lord, and he will lift you up[5]

He is saying, "*Do anything, do whatever it takes. But give Jesus your whole life! Anything else is a total waste, and just gets in the way*".

A commitment to sin is like putting up a hand to God and saying, "*Back away! This part of my life is mine!*"

But, of course, such an act can only cloud the relationship. It gets in between you and your God, hampering the intimacy and power of your walk. When we put our hand up like that, it is, according to James, like telling a jealous lover to turn away while we sleep with someone else.

But to the humble, James says, God gives ever-increasing grace. We literally go from glory to glory when we choose a path of surrendered humility rather than stiff-necked pride.

As we commit to drawing near to God, He in turn draws near to us. He wants to engage with those that want Him. He won't impose, or deprive you of a value-driven choice.

The power so many seek for a supernatural life is most easily accessed through humble surrender. The grace is there for us, on offer for whoever would lay aside their own agendas and passionately pursue the face of God alone.

To the humble, like the woman caught in adultery, Jesus' hand lifts our chin to look directly at Him. There is no condemnation in those eyes – His desire is not to judge. He wants you, not your performance or achievements.

And Jesus wants you to want that too.

First prize is an intimate, continual and grace-giving relationship with God. It is a walk that is naturally supernatural. It is a dialogue about how to release the influence of the kingdom, not a monologue about life's problems.

This is what Jesus died for.

He didn't die to fix the world or overthrow empires. He didn't intend to renew everything just yet. These things, as incredibly important as they are, are all a distant second to Jesus' idea of first prize.

You.

Prayer

Lord, today I personalize the exhortation of Hebrews 12:1–3:

*Therefore, since I am surrounded by such a great
cloud of witnesses, I will throw off everything that
hinders and the sin that so easily entangles.*

*And I will run with perseverance the race
marked out for me, fixing my eyes on you Jesus,
the pioneer and perfecter of my faith.*

*For the joy set before you, You endured the cross, scorning
its shame, and sat down at the right hand of the throne of
God. I therefore consider you who endured such opposition
from sinners, so that I will not grow weary and lose heart.*

Amen.

REFERENCES

1. James 2:24
2. John 7:4–5
3. Jon 20:29
4. James 4:5
5. James 4:9–10

YOUR RESPONSE

Do you want what Jesus wants? After all you have been reflecting on these last weeks, what is your desire now?

Spend some time writing out what you long for in your life with God.

_____

_____

_____

_____

_____

_____

_____

_____

_____

_____

_____

_____

_____

_____

_____

_____

6.2

Walking in union

READ FIRST: JOHN 17

Did you notice that Jesus did not pray that you would become more holy?

Do you need more holiness? Of course, but that is a natural result of the thing that matters most – the thing Jesus *did* pray for.

Union.

He wants to be joined with you so closely that you are one. And once that is working well, He plans that you are joined with other believers in a unity that confounds all who lack it.

Love God totally ... and in the wake of that you will love people naturally.

This was to be your signpost to the world that God is real. Not an apologetic, not a miracle, not a perfect life – union with Christ. Achieve that and everything else we become so frenetic about tends to take care of itself.

It is significant that the disciples actually walked with Jesus for three years and yet never really got what He was about. They were with Him, but they were not in union with Him.

It wasn't until He ascended and they were full of the Spirit that they understood Jesus' agenda, and dedicated themselves to it.

Jesus was all about engaging with people and meeting their needs. The disciples seemed to vacillate between a fixation on Jesus overthrowing Rome and their backroom lobbying to be the most important in whatever leadership structure He would set up.

Not much has changed.

We do exactly the same thing when we associate ourselves with Jesus but don't live in union with Him.

We ask for His blessing in our life – to elevate our cause and to take away our inconvenience. We ask Him to open doors to make our life significant. We come to Him like James and John, "... *Jesus we want you to do for us what we ask*"[1]. We spend much of our life completely missing the point.

But when we are unified in spirit with Christ, everything changes. Everything.

Our perspective, our priorities, even the power in our life dramatically shift when we see with His eyes and touch the world with His hands.

Consider Peter and John in Acts 3, immediately after they are filled with the Spirit. As they came across the lame man, their response was different to what it had been in the past. Previously they would try to send people away rather than meet their needs.

On the hills of Galilee, they had tried to dismiss needy crowds, aware more of their own lack than of Jesus' unlimited provision. But in their new context of union with Christ, they stop next to a man they had probably passed many times before.

This time, rather than awareness of lack, they have an awareness of what they do have: Jesus within. *"What we have, we give you ... rise up and walk"*[2].

The disciples were no more holy than they were a few days previously. But their perspective, and therefore their power, had changed.

They were more like Jesus because they were walking in union with Him, not because they were more holy.

Think again about the reason you are reading this book and what it is equipping you for. The spiritual person, the *pneumatikos,* is one who is led by the Spirit. This is simply a description of a life in union with Christ.

The goal of the process you have been through is simple – walk like Jesus walked.

To do that you firstly repent, choosing to think in line with the way God thinks about yourself and Him. Secondly, you surrender to Him, believing that His way is better and He will give you what you need to do it.

How will you know when you are getting it right? That is easy; you will walk like Jesus.

What frustrated you yesterday will cease to do so. What incited your desire previously will lose its appeal. The thought of doing anything that would damage your relationship or hamper your union becomes deplorable.

Love God more than anything else and you will not pursue those lesser things. God's power within us is given to do what Jesus would do, not what our carnal nature would want Him to do.

When we make the turn *from* what we previously held dear, it is profound to see what we naturally turn *to.* More often than not, those who surrender their life to Christ find themselves with a deep compassion and priority for people. Just as Jesus did.

Suddenly they have eyes and time for others. Where they were previously impatient and intolerant, they now have a heart to listen and pray. They are not as flustered by interruptions, or resentful of those who block their path.

This is the work of God's Spirit within us.

When the world loses its grip on us, we seem to fall into the arms of people.

And yet, this is not a dynamic that can be manufactured. It is not like you can shortcut a step saying, "*I need to be more like Jesus, so I will give my life to the needs of people*". This mistake is the classic overreach of those who ultimately suffer the burnout from compassion fatigue.

You can only give of what you genuinely possess.

Love for people is often the most visible fruit of our love for God. But that fruit is sourced from a power deep within.

> *Remain in me, as I also remain in you. No branch can bear fruit by itself; it must remain in the vine. Neither can you bear fruit unless you remain in me.*

> *I am the vine; you are the branches. If you remain in me and I in you, you will bear much fruit; apart from me you can do nothing*[3].

Jesus is both the example of how life should look and the power to make that life possible. Your goal then is simple – turn to Him, defer to Him, join with Him and walk with Him.

PRAYER

Lord, once more I turn to you.

I turn my heart and affection to you. I praise who you are and worship you with my life.

I turn my priorities and plans to be yours. Help me see what you see and feel what you feel for this world.

Lord, join with me ever deeper today.

Amen.

REFERENCES

1. Mark 10:35
2. Acts 3:6
3. John 15:4–5

YOUR RESPONSE

Does the picture of life described in this chapter appeal to you? What is the response of your heart to the idea that the well-being of people becomes more of a priority than the agendas of this world?

_____

_____

_____

6.3

Heart of flesh; face like flint

READ FIRST: LUKE 9:51–62

Isaiah once prophetically spoke the words of Jesus saying, "*Because the Sovereign LORD helps me, I will not be disgraced. Therefore, have I set my face like flint, and I know I will not be put to shame*"[1].

Once Jesus realised it was time to initiate the sequence to the cross, He was resolute.

He wasn't sidetracked by the rejection of villages. He refused to offer cheap seats to the salvation dinner.

"*I am about to give everything I have; I expect you to do the same or walk away*".

His heart was still soft, but his face was like flint. Nothing would get Him off track now.

In the absence of a clear vision we invert this formula. Our hearts turn to stone and our faces wander to-and-fro. In our lack of determination, we end up with a calloused soul.

But now and again God arrests us again.

Imagine Jesus walking past your village on the way to the cross, the disciples scurrying along behind trying to keep up. He looks at you and stops. The same hunter's gleam that spotted Zacchaeus is now focused on you.

"The time has come," he says. *"The kingdom of God has come near to you. You can reach out and grab it. Repent and believe the good news!"*

What will you do now?

You know what Jesus means. Every word in those short sentences has been explained to you in this book. He didn't suggest you pray about it first. You don't need to analyse it in the original language, or have another focus group.

The situation is clear and immediate – you need to choose. Yes or no. In or out.

You know beyond doubt what matters most – union with Christ – seeking first His kingdom. You know there are things in your life that get in the way of that. Do they matter more than Jesus right now, or will you just set your face like flint and deal with them?

You can see the faces of those around you. There are the disciples, following Him whatever the cost. They are the true children of God, ready to grow their Father's dominion. They are people of honour and sacrifice.

But there are others. The "rich young rulers" of the day. They couldn't turn away from their idols, so they turned away sad from Jesus instead.

Who do you see yourself as – a son, or a slave?

> *Because you are his sons, God sent the Spirit of his Son into our hearts, the Spirit who calls out, "Abba, Father." So you are no longer a slave, but God's child; and since you are his child, God has made you also an heir.[2]*

Seeing yourself as a child of God incites a certain response to any awareness that something is between you and Him. It goes something like this: *"I am not that person! I am not putting up with this anymore!"*

If that is you, then it's time to set your face like flint – it is your moment to take steps in the right direction.

Step one is to ask, *"What needs to change?"*

Asking God is the quickest way to figure this out. He is normally quite immediate in His response to any question such as, *"What blockage is between you and me, Lord?"* Union with Christ is His first priority too, so the transfer of ideas on this aligned conversation can be fast.

Step two is to ask, *"Why does it need to change?"*

This question solidifies in our hearts the reasons why staying the same is an unacceptable option. We might conclude that *"This habit is destroying my soul"*, or that *"To carry on like this is hurting people and the heart of God"*.

Thirdly, we should ask both God and ourselves, *"What is the problem?"*

The fruit is easy to spot, but the root is the real issue to address. So we need to find the answers to questions like these: *"What need am I trying to meet?"*, *"What ungodly goal is being blocked?"*, *"What idol am I bowing to – and why?"*, *"What slave driver is cracking their whip over my head?"*

Fourthly, we should ask, *"What will it look like when the change has taken place?"*

This often neglected step gives us a clear picture of a preferred future. Without that, we tend to lose momentum in the process of transformation. We need to know that the discomfort is worth it and that there is an end to this journey we are taking.

A dream that we believe is attainable, combined with a few intentional steps of progress, is an incredibly motivating combination.

To make this process easier for you, there is a simple Plan to Change at the back of this book[3].

The four questions that have just been explained make up the first part of that plan. Once we are clear on what needs to change and why, we are ready to create a path forward to a better future.

Take some time now to fill those questions out. Do not try to do any more just yet. In the next chapter you will learn how to make your preferred future a reality.

But before you begin, pray one more time …

PRAYER

Lord, what is blocking my relationship with you? What needs to change in my life for me to realise more fully my union with you?

Amen.

REFERENCES

1. Isaiah 50:7
2. Galatians 4:6–7
3. Appendix 2: A Plan to Change

YOUR RESPONSE

Today, spend time filling out the first four questions in your Plan to Change – Appendix 2, at the back of this book.

_____

_____

_____

_____

_____

_____

_____

_____

_____

_____

_____

_____

_____

_____

_____

How did Jesus grow people?

READ FIRST: LUKE 10:1–24

Do you remember some of the key times in your walk with God that the rate of growth seemed the fastest?

Think back on those seasons. What was happening in you, or perhaps to you, that resulted in you growing as you did?

Was it hardship that forced you to stretch in your endurance and thinking? Was it the input of a mentor or friend who gave you wisdom and support? Perhaps it was a sovereign work of God in your heart that opened your eyes and ignited your passion?

There are all sorts of external and internal triggers for development. And depending on our stage of life, maturity, responsiveness and personality, different elements will have a different impact.

Most growth is not sought after on our part. People normally avoid development unless it clearly facilitates their own agenda. That's because growth requires change, which results in discomfort. And who would choose to be uncomfortable, right?

Jesus' primary goal for life is not to make you comfortable, otherwise He would have fixed the world and made ice-cream a major source of vitamins.

His goal is that you come to life and dwell in union with Him. It was so important that He was prepared to die to make that possible.

As the Master Teacher, Jesus knew how to catalyse growth. When He sent out the 72 followers, it was a deliberate move to mature them somewhat. He had done it previously with the 12, but here He was taking the opportunity to expand the team to another tier.

We can see from His methods that there was a deliberate yet simple strategy, and also a good degree of success. There are dynamics of growth in His plan that are universal and effective. So let's break it down and identify how Jesus did it.

The first thing to notice was that He didn't simply teach them. He sent them out to new places that would stretch their faith and comfort.

This brought an element of context to the environment in which they grew. So, we can note that context and content combine powerfully if they are both applied in balance. We often think that receiving the right teaching should be enough to change us. And so we subscribe to endless podcasts and attend conferences, hoping for the missing pearl of wisdom that will unlock our next breakthrough.

As we look at how Jesus grew people, and how He grows you, you will see that instruction plays a part, but the ratio of content to context is far less than we might assume. Let's begin with context. Within that genre we see three elements of growth.

SPIRITUAL

Jesus gave the 72 a degree of spiritual authority that they did not have previously. In this pre-Pentecost environment, Jesus would draw down from heaven and imbue these people with the upgrade required to do more than attempt to convince people to embrace the kingdom. They were able to demonstrate God's power, not just talk about it.

When it comes to our development, remember that 2 Corinthians 3:18 validates spiritual experiences in the transformational process. As we contemplate God's glory, we grow in glory that can only come from His Spirit.

EXPERIENTIAL

Jesus sent them to do a practical task. They would go into an environment that forced them to engage with life, not just theory. They would potentially encounter hunger, persecution, disappointment as well as success. But that success wouldn't come from conquering an app or solving an equation on a whiteboard; they were to engage in the dust and sweat of real people's push-back and need.

Jesus will use life's experiences to grow you. The people and challenges around us that we often pray for Him to remove might be the very elements He wants to use to grow you.

RELATIONAL

Jesus' followers were sent out in pairs, and they were sent to real people. Our 21ˢᵗ century Western life has presented us with the option of doing most of our work remotely, or via social media, or in a closed room gazing at a screen. When those who are introverted and task oriented seek to fulfil God's will in their life, they will default to doing it in that environment.

But God doesn't want you to connect with virtual reality, Facebook or computer code. You are designed to engage with other human beings. It is relationships that change people. They need to see your eyes and look into your heart.

If you dwell on the seasons of growth you have experienced so far, it would be rare not to have a face and name or two attached to that process. We grow best when we grow with people.

These first three elements make up the context in which we grow. Finally, we can observe that content too plays a part.

INSTRUCTIONAL

Jesus had clear instructions and parameters for His followers to adhere to. These guidelines, like river banks that keep the flow of water in the right direction, are obviously a crucial part of the development process.

Good thinking, accurate theology and practical wisdom will always be important in our growth. Romans 12:2 clearly states that we are transformed by the renewing of the way we think. We just need to be aware that truth alone will not change us in the absence of obedience.

These then make up the four categories of growth that we can refer to in our transformational journey.

Applying them well can ensure that our Plan for Growth will develop us a whole person, thus ensuring that change is for the most part permanent.

PRAYER

Lord, I am amazed at the ways in which you have grown me. Thank you for using people and place, teaching and grace to change me in ways I could not have imagined. Keep growing me Lord, and show me your ways, so I might cooperate with you more, rather than work against your plans.

Amen.

REFERENCES

For more information on the four dynamics of development mentioned in this chapter, refer to the works of Malcolm Webber, available through www.leadersource.org

YOUR RESPONSE

Think of your past experiences of growth in life. Which of the four elements came in to play, and how did they result in transformation?

_____

_____

_____

_____

_____

_____

_____

6.5

Form a strategy

Your spiritual health is exactly where you want it to be.

Sure, life provides us a myriad of setbacks, traumas and challenges that impact our hearts, but ultimately we retain the choice for how we respond to that over the long term. God made us with a capacity to choose, and He will not take that away from you.

Seldom does one choice in itself transform us fully, although that does happen. Normally the choices that matter most are those that keep us on the journey of transformation. Abundant life comes to us gradually, and that in itself is a heroic journey.

The condition of your inner world, not what has happened to you circumstantially, determines the ultimate state of your life.

Jesus' parable of the sower illustrates that. The same seed of the kingdom falls on every soil, but the resultant growth depends on the condition of the soil itself.

You are that soil.

The composition of our thought life and heart has a huge impact on why some people seem to flourish through incredible hardship, while others gripe at the least of troubles.

We aren't all great at self-assessment of what ails us. Introspection does not come easily to all, and it seldom results in a positive outcome. Too often it ends in us feeling bad about ourselves, or in endless circular thoughts that bring no outcome.

We need a circuit-breaker.

We can break the cycle by re-framing the questions we ask about ourselves. Rather than ending the internal conversation with, *"What is the problem with me?"* we should move on to ask, *"What do I need?"*

Each soil that Jesus mentions in the Parable of the Sower can be rectified. Thorns can be weeded out, hardness can be softened rocks can be removed, and nutrients can be added.

If you have a preferred picture in mind of how life can and should look for you – and that picture lines up with what the Bible says – then you can be sure God has exactly what you need to make that picture a reality.

As James 4:6 says, God gives us more grace as we humbly seek the provision God has for us. And Peter agrees in 2 Peter 1:3, telling us:

> *His divine power has given us everything we need*
> *for a godly life through our knowledge of him*
> *who called us by his own glory and goodness.*

> *Through these he has given us his very great and*
> *precious promises, so that through them you may*
> *participate in the divine nature, having escaped the*
> *corruption in the world caused by evil desires.*

God does not withhold what we need. It is all around us if we seek it out. The grace we need comes in many forms, not all of them through supernatural experience or filling of the Spirit.

He has designed us to be spiritual, physical, relational and intellectual beings. As such, all of those elements of our life need to be nurtured and grown.

Like soil, we are organic in nature, not strictly segmented off with clear walls between these areas. Toxic relationships can damage our heart, bad thinking can affect our physical condition, and vice versa.

As we seek to grow in an area, the answer to the question "*What do I need?*" can helpfully be addressed to these four areas. We saw in the previous chapter that Jesus grew His followers by connecting them with something new through these four dynamics.

SPIRITUAL

This dynamic connected them with God through His Spirit. God is Spirit and interacts with us primarily at that level. Grace, God's empowering presence, gives us healing, adoption, identity, security, encouragement, peace, enlightenment, deliverance and strength.

The Spiritual dynamic connects us with God. To develop an area of life where we are lacking, we can validly enquire as to what grace we need from God. We can then, with confidence and expectancy, embrace that provision.

Invariably, that specific grace will most readily take effect if we connect our development with the remaining elements.

EXPERIENTIAL

As physical beings, we cannot limit our development or healing to the realm of our inner worlds. We need to integrate our hearts, heads and hands so that we are not living outwardly in contradiction to what we are trying to develop inwardly. We need to do that which agrees with the way we think.

The Experiential dynamic connect us with life. We have been placed in this world to engage with and physically sense it. The disciples were sent out into that world to experience push-back and victory. They were stretched beyond their comfort zone to do what they would not have initiated on their own. In doing so they grew.

Often, the grace we seek through God's Spirit is most evidently appropriated in the midst of a real-world experience. He provides as we need it, not in advance to be stored up.

When considering your growth, ask yourself, *"What experiences do I need to go through?"*

RELATIONAL

God's creation could only be described as *"very good"* once there was more than one person. We are designed to engage with people. That engagement includes tangible give and take as we understand that we are incomplete without each other.

As impressive as a single person can be, God has made us an inter-dependent community where we add to the strengths and compensate for the weaknesses of others.

The Relational dynamic connects us with people. The disciples were sent out in pairs, they did life together, they engaged with real people and problems.

What people do you need in your life right now? Are there mentors, peers, or even those you should be helping that need to be added to your life?

INSTRUCTIONAL

The most powerful weapon in our spiritual and developmental arsenal is a mind that thinks clearly. The broader our understanding and scope of accurate knowledge, the more we are able to correct our rationale.

The Instructional dynamic connects us with truth. It is truth that sets us free[1], and when coupled with practical application through the other dynamics, knowledge is indeed power.

What might you need to learn? What lies need to be exchanged with truth? Where would you get that instruction, and for how long?

These are the questions of a true learner.

So now, as you come to form a strategy for growth, consider these four dynamics. Which ones might particularly help you right now to grow where you need to?

PRAYER

Lord, as I come to plan the next stage of my growth, give me wisdom and clarity to identify what it is that I need. You have created me to draw from many sources; lead me to those that will bring life to me.

Amen.

REFERENCES

  1. John 8:32

YOUR RESPONSE

Go **Appendix 2: A Plan for Change**. Consider the area in which you want to grow, and think through how each area might hold a key for your next stage.

Begin then to write in some ways in which you can plan for growth.

_____

_____

_____

_____

_____

_____

Take a step

READ FIRST: MATTHEW 14:14–36

What would you have done if you were in the boat that evening on Lake Galilee.

It is hard to imagine a setting where reality would be more intense, or unreal. Saturated, scared and tired, the disciples were probably on the edge of rationality as it was, but then Jesus strolled up to them on top of the waves.

How would you respond?

What would you have done when you saw Peter leap off the side, taking more initiative than anyone else was prepared to show?

Of course, being the first person to try, Peter was also the first to fail. When you are a leader, it goes with the territory.

Those who merely sit back and observe are happy to conduct the post-mortem on what Peter should have done differently.

The view is always much clearer from the spectators' seats.

However, those who stayed in the boat were locked in an old way of thinking, unable yet to bend. The previous day they had seen the impossible – thousands of hungry people fed by a few pieces of bread and a couple of fish.

They had isolated that experience in a benign way, and in doing so had missed the point. The miracle was a signpost to a higher principle; that is, that God thinks outside of the box when it comes to meeting our needs. In his account of the same night, Mark's gospel says that the disciples were amazed that Jesus walked on water because they did not grasp the message sent by the loaves and fishes[1].

But for Peter it was a mini-*kairos* moment – an opportune time to try a different path. In the same way that you have consulted Jesus about a new way, Peter was given the green light.

"Can I do this Lord?" we ask. *"Is it ok?"*

"Of course you can, in fact I was hoping you would give it a try".

And so, over the side he went. It started well, because His eyes were locked on Jesus. When we see things from God's viewpoint, anything is possible.

You are at that point now.

You have seen your *kairos* moment, you have made a plan, and now it is time to take a step over the side of the boat you have been struggling in.

What is your first step?

Who do you need to talk to? What do you need to do?

Enthusiasm thrives on progress towards a plan. It energises us when we take our first positive step. Doing nothing to move forward when we know we should and could is debilitating to our self-esteem and motivation.

So determine your first step, be it ever so small, and take it today.

Now, it is said that the first step is the hardest. But I think that is debatable.

In Peter's case, it wasn't the first step that he got wrong, he did that really well. It was the steps that followed. As soon as he took his eyes off Jesus, and on to all the reasons why his walk was impossible, he disconnected from the miraculous.

Be ready for this!

Once you get past the initial decision to change your path, all the forces of life that conspired to keep you stuck in the old way will push back on you. The relational tensions, the work situation, the frailty of your heart – they are all still there when you decide you need to change.

This is why you need faith – it is the belief after repentance that holds most of the power to change.

When we are reminded of the ongoing presence of the wind and waves that have kept us in the boat, it can destroy our faith.

God is stronger than all that, and His power in us is more than enough to overcome. But if our perspective and rationale revert back to our old ways, then we disengage from that grace.

Remember, all things are available and yet not automatic.

And so, take your first steps today and be ready for the next steps tomorrow. Have a strategy in place for the inevitable doubt that will flood your mind. Emotional triggers from the presence of certain people will tug at you again – deny their authority over you. Neural pathways in your physical brain will draw your thoughts back to old thinking.

You are better than that. The world and your old nature have no right to tell you who you are, what you are worth and what you can do. God reserves that right, and He has placed within you the same power that raised Jesus from the dead. Therefore, the limits are off!

And if the Spirit of him who raised Jesus from the dead is living in you, he who raised Christ from the dead will also give life to your mortal bodies because of his Spirit who lives in you.

Therefore, brothers and sisters, we have an obligation— but it is not to the flesh, to live according to it.²

Peter did fail. This time.

You may have set backs too. But that doesn't mean the process is not working or that you will not get there.

The only way to fail is to disengage from the journey altogether. God is faithful even when you are not. He lifted Peter from the sea, and He will always lift you too.

Do you think He is committed to you less, now that you are saved, than He did when you were a sinner?

Jesus promised that *"I am with you always, even to the end of the age"³*.

All He asks is that we take a walk with Him, beginning with a step in the right direction. It doesn't matter if you have failed a million times. If you choose His way now, then you are on the track He wants for you right now.

So keep your eyes on Christ – and take a step today that will bring you closer to Him.

PRAYER

Lord, thank you for always lifting me up and giving me another chance. I can only stand on the stormy waters by your grace. Help me to believe in you more and more each day.

Thank you for all I have learned, and hope to apply each day.

I am yours, Lord; take me and do what you will!

Amen.

REFERENCES

1. Mark 6:51–52
2. Romans 8:11
3. Matthew 28:20

YOUR RESPONSE

What is the step you will take today to initiate your journey
into transformation?

_____

_____

_____

_____

_____

_____

_____

_____

_____

_____

_____

_____

Group Session 7

This course has invited you into a Christ-centred life, rather than a moral-centred life. Some might assume that our personal transformation is all about behaving better. Living morally is a good thing, but it is second prize – one of many second prizes in Christian living.

First prize is deep union with Christ. Live this way and, as Jesus says, the rest comes naturally. Morality is much more of a fruit of our union with Christ than it is a route to that union.

> *"But seek first his kingdom and his righteousness, and all these things will be given to you as well"*. (Matthew 6:33)

Q. What was your overall response to this week's content?

_____

_____

_____

_____

_____

Your Plan to Change

Share together your responses to this week's material, and the detail of your Plan to Change.

_____

_____

_____

_____

_____

_____

_____

_____

Re-assess

Now, re-look at **Part 1 of Appendix 1: Spiritual Health Assessment**, responding to the rating matrix of **Spiritual and Emotional Maturity**.

_____

_____

_____

_____

How have your responses changed since the beginning of this material?

_____

_____

_____

_____

_____

_____

_____

_____

What has been the greatest benefit of this material for you personally?

_____

_____

_____

_____

_____

_____

_____

_____

_____

_____

_____

_____

Pray for each other. And discuss whether you should continue to meet as a group to encourage and share progress.

Appendix 1:

SPIRITUAL HEALTH ASSESSMENT

PART 1: SPIRITUAL AND EMOTIONAL
MATURITY

Spiritual maturity is measured by our ability to follow the leadings of the Holy Spirit within us, and live from the nature and priority of Christ. In the following areas, **indicate how you rate out of 10**, and at the end of this course you will re-visit this assessment to see if you have grown.

1. I am aware daily of the Spirit's tangible help in my thoughts and actions.

As I begin this book		On finishing this book	
I rate myself at:	My friend/ spouse says:	I rate myself at:	My friend/ spouse says:

2. I am aware of and operate in the gifts of the Spirit fairly consistently.

As I begin this book		On finishing this book	
I rate myself at:	My friend/ spouse says:	I rate myself at:	My friend/ spouse says:

3. I have an intimate and clear ongoing relationship with God and hear His leadings.

As I begin this book		On finishing this book	
I rate myself at:	My friend/ spouse says:	I rate myself at:	My friend/ spouse says:

4. I find worship and thanksgiving a natural part of my life.

As I begin this book		On finishing this book	
I rate myself at:	My friend/ spouse says:	I rate myself at:	My friend/ spouse says:

5. When I am aware of an area to grow, I am equipped to follow that process.

As I begin this book		On finishing this book	
I rate myself at:	My friend/ spouse says:	I rate myself at:	My friend/ spouse says:

I take personal responsibility for my spiritual health and growth.

As I begin this book		On finishing this book	
I rate myself at:	My friend/ spouse says:	I rate myself at:	My friend/ spouse says:

6. I am aware, and people confirm, that I am growing in my spiritual walk.

As I begin this book		On finishing this book	
I rate myself at:	My friend/ spouse says:	I rate myself at:	My friend/ spouse says:

7. I am secure and at peace with who I am.

As I begin this book		On finishing this book	
I rate myself at:	My friend/ spouse says:	I rate myself at:	My friend/ spouse says:

8. I have control of my inner world and do not feel obliged to sin.

As I begin this book		On finishing this book	
I rate myself at:	My friend/ spouse says:	I rate myself at:	My friend/ spouse says:

9. When God convicts me to change, I recognise His grace to overcome.

As I begin this book		On finishing this book	
I rate myself at:	My friend/ spouse says:	I rate myself at:	My friend/ spouse says:

10. I am not entangled in the priorities of the world or the idols it puts in place of God.

As I begin this book		On finishing this book	
I rate myself at:	My friend/ spouse says:	I rate myself at:	My friend/ spouse says:

11. When God highlights an area of life to change, I know how to plan for growth.

As I begin this book		On finishing this book	
I rate myself at:	My friend/ spouse says:	I rate myself at:	My friend/ spouse says:

PART 2: OUR DAY-TO-DAY STRUGGLES

We all have areas where we are yet to break through. Use this exercise to help you identify them.

Key to answers.

0	1	2
This is not something I experience	I slip in this area occasionally but not regularly	So far I have not been able to overcome this

		0	1	2
1	I struggle with feelings of inadequacy.			
2	I feel a strong burden of having to provide well for my family.			
3	I find myself secretly competing with the people around me.			
4	I tend to build cases against people who seem successful or have power over me.			
5	I spend a lot of time wondering what people think about me.			
6	When people don't agree with me I take it personally and tend to think that they have rejected me.			
7	I am easily offended.			
8	I over-react when I feel judged.			
9	I lash out when my self-worth is threatened.			

10	I'm jealous when my partner talks to the opposite sex.			
11	I control who my partner sees and where they go.			
12	I need to be in a relationship to feel OK.			
13	When I look at myself I am never satisfied.			
14	I struggle with body image.			
15	I hide how much I drink.			
16	I drink to get drunk.			
17	When I drink I always get tipsy or go overboard.			
18	I turn to drugs or medication to ease my inner struggles.			
19	I use food to cope with my feelings.			
20	Sometimes I want to hurt myself.			
21	I struggle with viewing pornography.			
22	I have gay thoughts and feelings.			
23	I have a problem with sex.			
24	I change my opinion to please other people.			
25	I feel compelled to argue with or manipulate people into agreeing with me.			
26	I feel I have been misunderstood most of my life.			
27	Sometimes I hit my partner when I get angry.			

28	I struggle to control my anger with those around me.			
29	I struggle to form relationships and trust others.			
30	I judge people often and it lessens my view of them.			
31	When I am angry at someone I want to hurt them in some way.			
32	I struggle with fears generally.			
33	I have a fear of rejection.			
34	I worry about the future.			
35	I have a fear of being inadequate or insignificant.			
36	I have a fear of failure.			
37	I often feel like something is about to go wrong.			
38	I overwork and feel really low when I am not accomplishing something.			
39	I am afraid to set goals because when I don't reach them, it makes me feel like I have failed.			
40	People think I am obsessed with being right.			
41	I do not know when to take a rest.			
42	A lot of the time I only feel good if I look my best.			
43	I feel ashamed about things I've done in the past.			

44	I can't forgive myself.			
45	I feel numb or even empty inside.			
46	Nothing I do is ever good enough.			
47	I only feel significant when I'm working.			
48	I only feel good about myself when I have been exercising.			
49	I feel like there's a ceiling between me and God.			
50	I want to win all of the time.			
51	I know what I'm doing is wrong but I can't seem to stop.			
52	I am not able to trust God to do what I need.			
53	I struggle to make decisions without God guiding me explicitly.			
54	I am a different person at home than I am at church, work or school.			
55	I have areas of my life I cannot talk about with anyone.			
56	When people get too close, I withdraw.			
57	I am afraid people will be disappointed if they saw the real me.			
58	I think God is angry with me because of my failures.			

Are there any other areas you would like to be able to address?

_____

_____

_____

_____

_____

_____

_____

_____

_____

_____

_____

_____

_____

_____

If you had to highlight one or two areas to deal with, what would they be?

_____

_____

_____

_____

_____

_____

_____

_____

_____

_____

_____

_____

_____

Appendix 2:

A PLAN TO CHANGE

WHAT NEEDS TO CHANGE?

_____

_____

_____

_____

_____

_____

_____

_____

_____

_____

WHY DOES IT NEED TO CHANGE?

_____

_____

_____

_____

_____

_____

_____

WHAT IS THE PROBLEM?

_____

_____

_____

_____

_____

_____

_____

WHAT WILL IT LOOK LIKE WHEN THE CHANGE
HAS TAKEN PLACE?

_____

_____

_____

_____

_____

_____

_____

WHAT DO I NEED?

In the following four areas, determine how you might need
input that will help transform your situation.

Spiritual dynamic – how do I need to connect with God?
Consider ways to engage more vibrantly, praise and worship genuinely, embrace His Spirit more powerfully.
Is there a way to measure progress?

Experiential dynamic – how do I need to connect with life?

Consider new places and practices to engage with that will stretch you where needed.

Is there a way to measure progress?

Relational dynamic – how do I need to connect with people?

Consider who might be able to support, guide, complement and encourage you.

Is there a way to measure progress?

Instructional dynamic – how do I need to connect with truth?

Consider what training or teaching would help you understand God, His ways and His grace more fully.

Is there a way to measure progress?

Printed in Australia
AUOC01n0423160317
283875AU00002BA/2/P